Temples
and
Tacos

Valerie Astill

PNEUMA SPRINGS PUBLISHING UK

First Published in 2011 by:
Pneuma Springs Publishing

Temples and Tacos
Copyright © 2011   Valerie Astill
ISBN: 978-1-907728-07-5

Pneuma Springs Publishing
A Subsidiary of Pneuma Springs Ltd.
7 Groveherst Road, Dartford Kent, DA1 5JD.
E: admin@pneumasprings.co.uk
W: www.pneumasprings.co.uk

A catalogue record for this book is available from the British Library.

A tour through Mexico, Guatemala and Belize

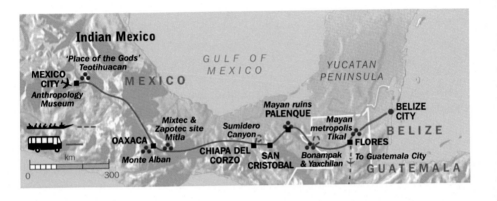

All names have been changed in the interests of privacy.

This book is dedicated to my husband, David, for his unfailing love, encouragement and support and for always being there for me.

My thanks go to Explore Worldwide who provided the holiday and, in particular, to Paul Bondsfield, who supplied the map and gave permission for this book to be published; and to William Potter, who went to the trouble of sending Explore photographs relating to this trip although, in the end, none of these was used.

My thanks also go to those who allow free reproduction of their photographs published on Wikipedia Commons, two of which have been included in this book.

1

Mexico City and the Aztecs

Saturday 28th June

"There's our other case," David said and, as it came round on the conveyor belt, he pulled it off and put it on the luggage trolley. It was the end of a very long journey. We had left home before dawn that morning to drive to Gatwick Airport before taking the 9.40 am flight to Houston, Texas. This had landed at 7.15 pm GMT, giving us less than an hour and a half before our flight to Mexico City. In that time, we had queued at Passport Control and cleared Customs to reach the Arrivals area, before immediately checking in again, passing through security and further passport controls to get to the Departure Lounge and boarding almost immediately. It was now about 5 pm local time, nearly 11 pm GMT, and we were shattered.

As we wheeled our luggage out through the 'Nothing to Declare' lane, a Customs Officer stepped out in front of us. "Bring your bags over here, please!" "Oh no," groaned David. "That's all we need." "We're part of a group," I pleaded, hoping the stern-looking official would relent and let us through, but to no avail. We took our luggage to a side table and watched while he emptied half the contents out of each of our carefully packed cases and rummaged through the remainder. "That's OK," he assured us, leaving everything spread across the table. He then wandered off to select another victim while we were left to repack the cases.

When we eventually went through to the Arrivals area, we found our Explore group leader, a short, stocky young man with blond spiky hair in his mid-twenties, waiting for us with three other people.

"Welcome," he said, "I'm Peter." He checked his list. "You must be David and Valerie Astill." We nodded. "You were the only ones we were still waiting for, so we'll head for the hotel." He took us outside where the six of us, plus all our luggage, somehow managed to squeeze into one taxi, David and Peter at the front, the rest of us in the back. We were soon on our way to the centre of Mexico City which, fortunately, was less than five miles away.

On the journey, we introduced ourselves and found out more about our fellow travellers. Sue in her mid-twenties, slim, dark-haired and very attractive, was a trainee solicitor from Brighton; Garry in his early thirties, with light brown hair and an infectious smile, was an engineer from Salisbury; while Ian in his early twenties, a very tall, gangly redhead, was an art student from Dunstable. "Sorry if we delayed you," David said apologetically, "but we were caught by Customs." "I saw them stop you," said Garry. "I was just thankful it wasn't me." "When they're not so busy, they pick out every one in ten passengers," Peter told us. "You were just unfortunate enough to be the tenth."

Our hotel, the Premier, was in a good central location just off the Paseo de la Reforma, one of the main roads through the city. Peter booked us in at Reception and handed us our room keys. "I'm meeting the rest of the group at 8 o'clock to go to a local restaurant," he said. "Would you like to join us?" "I hope you don't mind," said Sue, "but I feel too tired tonight." "Me too," I said. "It's nearly midnight UK time and we had an early start." The three men had also had enough for one day.

"I understand," said Peter. "Get a good night's sleep and I'll see you in the morning. Breakfast is served from seven o'clock in the restaurant at the back of the lobby. Bring your insurance documents down with you and I'll meet you here in the reception area at nine o'clock to check them over. There will then be a short briefing before we set off to visit the National Anthropological Museum. You can have lunch at the Museum and the afternoon will be free. I suggest you each bring a bottle of water with you. You'll find the heat and altitude make you very thirsty."

Up in our room, David went straight to bed and fell asleep almost immediately. As we would be staying at the Premier for three nights, I unpacked a few necessities and, trying to adjust to local time, managed to stay up until nearly 9 pm before succumbing and collapsing into bed.

Sunday 29th June

Despite our exhaustion the previous evening, I was wide awake again at 3 am due to jetlag. After trying unsuccessfully to drop off again, I turned over and saw David sitting up in bed. "I can't sleep," he complained. "Neither can I. Do you fancy a hot drink?" We made use of the kettle, tea and coffee provided, ate the two little packets of complimentary biscuits and read the books we had brought with us to pass the time, although we found it difficult to concentrate. As soon as it began to get light, I said, "I'm going to get ready and go out for a walk." "Wait until I've had a shower and shave and I'll come with you."

It was about 6 am by the time we left the hotel to explore our immediate surroundings. We were in an area of concrete skyscrapers that were functional rather than attractive and only a few minutes walk from the Paseo de la Reforma, a wide main road with three traffic lanes in either direction, separated by a small band of greenery down the centre. "It's a bit fresh," I said shivering. "We'd better go back soon," said David, "I don't want you getting cold." He suddenly exclaimed, "What's that?" as a tiny green hummingbird hovered in front of us for a few seconds. "It's a hummingbird," I said, thrilled, and immediately forgot about the chill in the air.

Back in our hotel room, we sorted out our insurance documents and we were soon downstairs again, waiting outside the restaurant when it opened for breakfast at 7 am. We helped ourselves from the buffet and while we were eating, the rest of the group gradually filtered in. We introduced ourselves to those we had not already met, all of whom had arrived on earlier flights the day before.

Neville and Diane from Canada were in their early fifties, a little younger than David and I. Neville, an accountant, was dark-haired with a short, neatly trimmed beard. He was of medium height, broad and stocky and beginning to develop a slight paunch. Diane, a teacher, was slightly shorter than her husband, plump and motherly and with black hair rolled into a French pleat. With them was their daughter Kayleigh, a slim, dark-haired girl, bouncing with energy and enthusiasm, who appeared to be in her late teens. There were also two young couples in their twenties from Australia. Cheryl and Sam had been married for two years and lived in the Northern Territory where Sam was a miner. He was a large, well built man, about six foot three inches tall with long untidy brown hair, beard and moustache while Cheryl, another teacher, was slim, about five foot ten inches tall and a redhead, her long hair neatly tied back in a ponytail. They had already made firm friends with Lynn and Alan from Melbourne, who were a little younger than Cheryl and Sam and had only met the previous year at University. They were both slim and of medium height but Alan had light brown hair, while Lynn was an attractive blonde who wore spectacles, which made her look studious. They were still living at home with their respective parents and this was their first holiday together. The group was completed by Sonia from Gibraltar, a small, trim office worker with short dark curly hair, who appeared to be in her early forties.

After breakfast, we all bought bottled water, collected our bags from our rooms and at 9 o'clock, met back in the lobby where Peter was waiting. He quickly checked our insurance documents to make sure we all had adequate cover and then, while we sat and relaxed on the comfortable leather sofas, he gave us a brief overview of the holiday itinerary and handed each of us a photocopied map of the city centre on which he had highlighted our hotel. He was just finishing when a large man in his early fifties, with curly greying hair and a friendly face, came striding into the lobby. Peter introduced him. "This is our local guide, Joseph. He's our expert on Mexico City and will be with us for the next two days."

Joseph beamed at us. "Welcome to Mexico City," he said. "This morning, we shall be visiting the National Anthropological Museum to give you an introduction to the history of Mexico, so that you have a better understanding of what you will see later on your tour. Please come with me."

We followed Joseph out of the hotel and down to the Paseo de la Reforma where we stood and waited at a bus stop, enjoying the warmth of the sunshine and the rapidly rising temperatures. "It's getting hot already," commented David. Joseph had just started to tell us about the traffic and pollution problems in the city when a bus came along and we all boarded. "I'll pay the fares," said Peter. "We're only going a short distance." A few minutes later, we were getting off the bus at Chapultepec Park, situated at the other end of the Paseo de la Reforma.

"Be very careful how you cross the road," cautioned Joseph. "The traffic is very heavy in the mornings." We went across to the park and the National Anthropological Museum which stood just inside the entrance. A broad flight of shallow steps led up to the low grey concrete building, its severity relieved by a few trees and shrubs, four fountains playing in a pool in front of the entrance and the red, white and green flag of Mexico gently billowing from its flagpole.

We climbed the steps, walked through the entrance doors and found that it was pleasantly cool inside. The museum was built on two floors round a central open courtyard. Joseph went to buy the tickets and came back to us in the foyer. "You may take your bags round with you but please put your cameras away. Photographs of the exhibits are forbidden," he warned us. "There are eleven rooms on the ground floor, covering the periods from Prehistory to the arrival of the Spaniards in 1519 and I shall be taking you round these this morning."

Joseph then handed out the tickets. "Keep these somewhere safe," he advised, "and then, if you want to, you'll be able to visit the galleries upstairs this afternoon without having to pay the entrance fee again." "What is there to see upstairs?" asked Sue. "Exhibits relating to the various tribal groups in existence today," he replied.

The museum was a wonderful introduction to the history of Mexico. The first known inhabitants were nomadic hunters who crossed from Siberia during the last Ice Age from as long ago as 50,000 BC, those settling in North America becoming the ancestors of the Eskimos and Native American Indians. By about 20,000 BC, the nomads had reached Mexico where, over time, those who settled became less dependent on hunting and began to grow crops. Pottery remains dating from about 2,300 BC had been found buried under village homes as offerings to the dead, together with clay female figurines related to fertility rituals and tools made of stone and bone.

Between about 1200 BC and 400 BC, a race of people known as the Olmecs occupied a lowland area towards the south of the Gulf of Mexico. They left behind them huge basalt sculptures, up to three metres high, of human heads apparently wearing helmets. Joseph pointed out their wide flat noses and thick lips. "These suggest that they originated from Africa," he said. "One of the gods they worshipped was a feathered serpent and their religious beliefs probably influenced those of the later Aztecs, who also had a feathered serpent god."

Around 300 BC, the mountainous Monte Alban region of Oaxaca was occupied by the Zapotecs. "The facial features of their stone carvings, known as Danzantes or dancers, have some similarities with the Olmec style," Joseph informed us. "They used writing and numbers based on hieroglyphs and a dot and bar system and they probably devised a calendar. Among their religious beliefs, they associated the jaguar with Earth and the Underworld while the serpent represented water and fertility."

Separate rooms of the museum were devoted to Olmecs, Zapotecs, Toltecs, Aztecs, Mixtecs and Mayans, the latter being the ancestors of most of the Indian tribes of Mexico today. One of the most fascinating rooms was the Teotihuacán Room, covering the period from 100 BC to 900 AD. As well as the expected exhibits of stone carvings and sculptures, pottery and jewellery, there was also the impressive reconstructed wall of a temple, finely sculpted and painted in vivid colours of red, orange, yellow, green and turquoise blue. "Teotihuacán covered an area of 40 square kilometres and when you visit the site tomorrow, you will be able to imagine how amazing this ancient city must have looked in its original colours," said Joseph. "Mineral colours were used on limestone plaster for buildings while vegetable dyes were used on cloth."

Further on, we came to a model of the city of Tenochtitlán. "Tenochtitlán was the origin of Mexico City and was built by the Aztecs between 1325 and 1345 AD," Joseph told us. "The Aztecs were once slaves of tribes who lived along the shore of a huge lake in the Valley of Mexico, called the Lago de Texcoco. One day these slaves rose up in rebellion against their masters and formed an army to fight the lakeside tribes and gain their freedom." "Didn't I read somewhere about them cutting off their enemies' ears?" queried Garry. "That's right," said Joseph. "The Aztecs won the battle and sent the tribal leaders eight thousand human ears as proof of victory, before leaving to found their own city. Aztec priests prophesised that on their journey, they would see an eagle standing on a cactus and eating a snake and that this would be the place where they should build their new city. As they walked across the marshes, they saw an eagle with a snake in its beak flying to one of the islands on the lake. It settled on top of a cactus plant, so that is where Tenochtitlán was founded."

As we walked round the museum, Joseph gave us more information than we could possibly absorb. We were thankful for the bottled water in our rucksacks as we found we needed to drink frequently. Our tour finished at lunchtime and we were then free for the rest of the day. David and I needed to sit and rest after standing around all morning so, although we were not really hungry, we went to the museum cafeteria for a light snack and discussed how we would spend the afternoon.

"Do you really want to see any more of the museum?" asked David. "I think I've had enough history and culture for one day." "We could use our map of the city centre and go exploring," I suggested. "No, my feet are tired with all that standing around," he said. "Let's just take it easy and wander round the park."

It was a hot, sunny Sunday and Chapultepec Park was crowded with families with young children. Paths of honey-coloured stone led through open woodland and grassy clearings. On one side of the path near the museum stood a row of stalls piled high with hot dogs, nuts, spicy snacks and delicious looking mixed fresh fruit, cubed and sliced in cellophane wrappers. While we were looking at these, a faint sound was carried on the breeze. "I can hear music," I said. "Let's walk in that direction and see what's happening."

We headed towards the centre of the park. "What on earth is that?" David suddenly exclaimed. I followed the direction of his gaze and above the tree canopy saw the top of a tall pole with what appeared to be four men spinning around it on the ends of ropes. We hurried in that direction and arrived at a large clearing between the trees, just in time to see the four men slowly circling the pole, close to the ground. They were dressed in white shirts and red trousers, each dangling upside-down, tied by one ankle to the end of a rope attached to the top of the pole. Once they stopped turning, other men came across and released them.

A young woman was standing near us with her two children so we asked her what it was all about. "It's an old tradition," she explained. "The men have to climb to the top of the pole and then they leap off and spin around until they reach the ground." It sounded like a cross between bungee jumping and a maypole dance. We guessed that it was the way the ropes were twisted round the pole beforehand that made the men spin round but the woman was unable to explain further. Before leaving, she warned us, "Don't eat any of the food on sale in the park unless you wash it first. The fruit looks tempting but it will make you ill." We thanked her for her advice.

As we continued through the park, we saw stalls selling toy windmills and a young man making model animals out of balloons and selling them to crowds of youngsters jostling to buy. Further along, children were lining up to have their faces painted. There was a choice of about ten designs, mostly involving spots and whiskers. This seemed to be the thing to do and we saw very few youngsters with unpainted faces, from toddlers in pushchairs to strapping early teenagers. The lakes were full of rowing boats jostling with paddle boats and long queues of people were awaiting their turn on the water, watched by families picnicking on the grass or standing around eating ice creams.

We followed the path gently uphill through a wooded area, where hammocks were for hire or sale. Quite a few people had slung hammocks between the trees and were snoozing in the shade.

Beyond the trees, we came to a high cliff where a castle towered above us. In the hillside beneath was the entrance to a Hall of Mirrors.

"Let's go and see the castle," I suggested. The road leading up to it looked quite steep but a train with open carriages was transporting people up the hill. We joined the queue but after we had been waiting for about fifteen minutes, a guard came along. "There will only be two more trains going up this afternoon," he said, counting from the front of the line and allocating people to the first or second train. "Sorry, that's all we can take today," he said to the rest of us.

"Is it worth walking up?" I asked the woman who had been in front of us in the queue with her daughter. "The building at the top was once a palace and is now a museum," she replied, "but it's quite a long way. It will probably be closed by the time you get there." "Let's go up a little way to see the view," suggested David. I thought that was a good idea and we started off.

There was plenty of shade to shield us from the afternoon sun but we had forgotten the effects of altitude. Mexico City is at a height of over two thousand metres or six and a half thousand feet and we were also suffering from jetlag and lack of sleep, so we were soon exhausted and decided it was too much effort. We looked over the wall across the park but although we were now above the tree canopy, there was little to see at that height other than foliage.

We made our way down again and wandered back to the park entrance near the Anthropological Museum. Just outside was what appeared to be a war memorial with three tall columns on either side. These columns were joined at the base by huge curved stone benches, each long enough to seat about twenty people and with stone back supports more than a metre high. As we sat resting our feet, we noticed in the distance the golden wings of an angel on top of the Monument of Independence, which Joseph had pointed out to us as we passed it in the bus that morning. "Do you want to take a bus back to the hotel or shall we walk?" I asked. "I think I'd rather walk than stand around again," decided David. "It can't be very far." "It doesn't look far on the map," I agreed.

As we made our way back along the Paseo de la Reforma, there were very few shops to look at. Most of the buildings were offices although we also passed some banks, blocks of flats and a few hotels and embassies, which looked very modern and stylish.

Rows of bunting were strung across the street, the flags covered in propaganda for the elections taking place the following week. The year was 1997, democracy was coming to Mexico and the citizens were being allowed to elect local mayors for the first time. There was some cynicism however. We started talking to a middle-aged couple who spoke excellent English and they told us that the ruling party had been in power for about thirty years and that before the last general election, the polls had forecast a runaway victory for the opposition. "On the day of the election, the computer systems recording the votes crashed, ballot boxes went missing and the ruling party remained in power," said the man despondently. "Many people are predicting trouble if the opposition loses again at the next general election, as we desperately need a change of government."

Back at the hotel, we showered and rested before meeting the group in the lobby to go out for the evening meal. Peter had decided to take us to a restaurant that was about half an hour's walk away. The food was good but David and I were too tired to eat very much. After the meal, most of the group went to explore the nightlife of Mexico City but we made our excuses and were very happy to return to our hotel to catch up on some sleep.

Monday 30th June

Jetlag woke us at 5 am, a little later than the previous morning. On our walk the day before, David and I had noticed a 24-hour café so we decided to go and have early breakfast. The food was excellent. After the meal, I walked a short way down the Paseo de la Reforma to photograph a monument I had noticed in the middle of the road, the statue of an Aztec warrior on a plinth wearing a long cloak and elaborate headdress with his spear raised, ready to throw. This was a memorial to Cuauhtemoc, the last Aztec emperor, who was executed by the Spaniard, Hernan Cortes, in 1525.

Back at the hotel, we had plenty of time to relax before meeting Peter and Joseph at 9 am for another day of sightseeing. Sonia joined the group late and looked really worried. "I've just been informed that my father, who's in his 80s, has been taken ill and rushed into hospital," she said. "They told me he was comfortable and out of danger but I'm wondering whether I should fly home today, while we're still in Mexico City." "If he's in hospital, he's in the best place and being well cared for," said Diane reassuringly. "As long as his condition remains stable, why not continue with your holiday for the time being but stay in regular touch with the hospital?" Other people in the group also encouraged her to stay and Peter assured her, "If you need to travel home from our next stop in Oaxaca, I can arrange this for you without any problem." She still seemed in two minds but agreed to think about it.

Our coach for the day was waiting outside the hotel and we were taken to the old centre of Mexico City. When we arrived, Joseph told us, "What little remains of the former lake bed is still drying out, at least partly due to extraction by the local water company. The whole of Mexico City is gradually sinking but this area is sinking faster than elsewhere. We are now going to see the remains of the Templo Mayor, the main temple of the ancient city of Tenochtitlán, which was built over the exact spot where the eagle with the snake settled on the cactus. The Aztecs regarded this as the centre of the world."

As we walked around the site, Joseph pointed out different phases of the temple building, the first temple having been constructed in the early 14th century. It was then built over and enlarged six times, each version being more elaborate than the previous one. The seventh version was what Cortes and his Spaniards found when they arrived in Tenochtitlán in 1519 AD.

"The Templo Mayor was dedicated to two Aztec gods, the God of War, Huizilopochtli, and the Water God, Tlaloc," explained Joseph. "The pyramid was forty metres high with four sloping tiers and had two stairways, one to each of the two shrines on the top platform, which was a hundred metres wide and eighty metres deep. Only the priests and those chosen for sacrifice were allowed to climb those stairs. At the top were sacred fires which were kept burning continuously. The pyramid would have been covered in limestone plaster with stucco designs painted in vivid colours."

As we were still trying to visualise this, we came to a large circular white stone, with deep carvings in the flat top surface depicting a dismembered female body, the torso in the centre being surrounded by the other body parts. "This is a replica of a stone carving of the Aztec Moon Goddess, Coyolxauhqui." Joseph told us. "She was murdered by her brother, Huizilopochtli, who also killed his four hundred brothers in order to become the leader of the gods. In 1978, workmen were digging to repair a telephone cable, damaged by sinking masonry. At a depth of about two metres, they discovered the original stone disk, more than three metres across, a third of a metre thick and weighing more than eight tons. Archaeologists knew that part of the foundations of the original Templo Mayor lay under the Cathedral, various finds having been made there since the end of the 19th century, but this discovery provided an opportunity to excavate an area to one side of it. Several old Spanish buildings were destroyed and work was only halted when the locals protested that the 16th century Spanish architecture was also part of their heritage."

Joseph then told us, "According to the Aztec calendar, Quetzalcoatl the feathered serpent, king of the gods, was expected to return to his people in 1519 AD, the year when the Spaniards, led by Cortes, reached the city of Tenochtitlán. Believing Cortes to be Quetzalcoatl, the Aztec king, Moctezuma, treated him with the greatest hospitality, housing him and his men in the Royal palace. The Spaniards rewarded his generosity by destroying the Aztec idols and trying to convert the people to Christianity. Increasing hostility on the part of the Aztecs led to war and Moctezuma was killed. The Spaniards fled the city but returned in 1521, by which time they were supported by a hundred thousand native Indians. This time, they defeated the Aztecs and captured Cuauhtemoc, the nephew of Moctezuma, who was now the ruler. The Spaniards razed the city of Tenochtitlán, destroying eighty Aztec pyramids, including the one in the Templo Mayor, before building Catholic churches on the Aztec foundations. We will now visit the Cathedral, which I think you will find very interesting."

Anthropological Museum, Mexico City

Circular Stone of Coyolxauhqui, Templo Mayor

Ancient rituals

Cathedral, Mexico City

As Joseph was leading us from the excavations to the nearby Cathedral, we saw on the pavement a collection of objects beside a semicircle of what looked like white blobs of candle wax, in one of which was planted the remains of a white candle. In the centre stood an upright cross of red flowers with sixteen rays of white flowers between the arms of the cross and further white flowers around the base. This was surrounded by all kinds of items, including containers holding bread, sugar and grains, a tomato, an egg, two glasses of milk and many objects which we did not recognise. Joseph hurried us past. "Don't go near that," he warned us. "It's part of an ancient ritual. It shows that the old gods are still worshipped."

We were crossing El Zocalo, the huge main square in front of the Cathedral, when we were passed by a group of soldiers in full uniform. "What's that they're carrying," wondered David. "It looks like a small barrel organ," I said, disbelievingly. Sure enough, it was. Rather incongruously, they set it up in a corner and began to play it.

Outside the Cathedral, we came to an enclosure and Joseph said, "This is the Fountain of Tenochtitlán." In the centre was a brass model of the Aztec city of Tenochtitlán, standing in a lake with causeways linking it to the shore. However, the effect was rather spoiled by the fact that it was being cleaned at the time by a workman with a long yellow broom and a bucket of water.

The Cathedral dominated the square and the outside of the building was magnificent. It was built of a light coloured stone, possibly limestone, and had two tall square bell towers, each capped with a bell-shaped roof, flanking a wide frontage with three baroque entrance arches. A clock tower rose above the centre portal, while set back behind this was a dome with a cupola and cross. To the right of this part of the building stood the sacristy, El Sagrario, its light stone facade flamboyantly carved and set off by triangular side walls like bookends, in contrasting red tezontle, a porous volcanic rock. Above this rose a second dome with a cupola and cross. As we entered this impressive building, however, we saw that the inside was a maze of scaffolding.

As Joseph led us round the Cathedral to show us some of the sixteen side chapels, the organ and the gilded Altar of the Kings behind the main altar, we passed between scaffolding poles which reached to the roof. Netting was stretched across to catch falling masonry and we felt as though we were walking round a building site. In one part of the building Joseph told us, "The Cathedral rests on a broken Aztec pyramid which is sinking unevenly, so the building is cracking and is four metres lower just here. Supports have been put under this corner in the hope that, as the rest of the building continues to sink, it will level up but because the sinking is uneven, the building will never be straight."

"The Cathedral has had other problems," he continued. "There are termites in the wall, eating away the masonry and, in 1967, a candle which was left burning overnight fell and started a fire. This was not discovered until the following morning, by which time most of the interior decoration had been destroyed. So far, it has taken eleven years to rebuild the organ and re-gild one altar." He added, "It was on this site that the invading Spaniards discovered more than one hundred and thirty thousand skulls of people sacrificed by the Aztecs. It is said that the Cathedral was built over the altar of the Sun God and that he will destroy it." "He seems to be making a successful job of it," commented Sam with a grin.

As we were leaving, Joseph stopped and pointed to a statue of the Madonna. "In the 16th century, the Virgin Mary was always shown standing on a crescent moon to represent the victory of Christianity over Islam," he said. "The Spaniards hoped to win the locals over to Christianity by trying to convince them that the new religion was almost the same as their own. They suggested to the Indians that Christ was the equivalent of their Sun God while the Virgin Mary was their Moon Goddess."

"This confusion still exists today," Joseph went on. "The Aztecs had about eight hundred different gods to cover all aspects of their day to day activities and in an attempt to convert them to Catholicism, the Spaniards tried to match each of these gods to a Catholic saint. Joseph became known as the Rain God and Francis of Assisi was seen as Quetzalcoatl. The practice continued and has grown over the years and today, Indian rituals are still practised in churches and there are church celebrations for two thousand different saints every year."

Neville looked puzzled. "That means that celebrations for several different saints would have to take place on the same day." "It doesn't work out that way," Joseph explained. "Many saints are local to particular villages or areas in different parts of the country and their feast days are only recognised locally."

We left the Cathedral and continued round the square. "The official name of the Zocalo is Constitution Square," Joseph told us. "It was once the site of an Aztec market and continued to be a market place until the early 20th century. The building in front of you is the National Palace, built by Cortes in 1523 on the site of the palace of Moctezuma, which he razed to the ground. It now houses the President's Office, the Treasury and the National Archives but part of the building is open for the public to view the paintings of Diego Rivera, dating back to the 1920s. These are what we are now going to see."

The National Palace extended across the full width of the square. We entered through the centre portal, above which hung a bell. "That bell is rung by the President of Mexico each year to commemorate the anniversary of Mexico's independence," Joseph told us, before turning to face the main staircase and a huge mural covering the wall behind, recording the history of Mexico City. Joseph pointed out the main areas of interest.

In the centre of the mural was the eagle standing on a cactus holding a snake in its beak. Below this, Aztecs were shown going about their daily business. In the upper part of the painting were the Cathedral with the fat bishops and archbishops. Diego Rivera also included the Spaniards, the French, who occupied Mexico for a few years during the 19th century, the unemployed, revolutionaries and guerrilla leaders, the whole painting being blended together in a masterpiece of planning.

We climbed the stairs and, on the upper floor, found a series of paintings depicting different aspects of the Aztec way of life before the Spaniards arrived. One showed how natural resources were used for food; for building houses and boats; and for making things as diverse as tools and clothing, parchment, inks, paints and dyes, pens and brushes.

21

"In this next painting, Rivera's woman friend is depicted as a high-class prostitute," said Joseph, pointing her out. "The man being carried in a sedan chair has been selected for sacrifice and as such, is highly honoured. His duty is to listen to everybody's problems and prayers for a year so that, when he is sacrificed at the end of the year, he can carry their messages to the gods. In the meantime, he is treated like a king and given everything he desires." "How was he chosen?" asked Diane. "People competed for that honour," replied Joseph. "Only the fittest and most skilled was acceptable for sacrifice."

Another painting showed the ceremonial side of life. In the foreground, priests in elaborate, brightly coloured robes and headdresses stood looking across to the pyramids and dancers. David and I were delighted to see that the painting included four pole spinners. They were dressed as eagles with their wings spread, spinning round the pole with the rope fastened around both feet. "We saw some men spinning round a pole like that in Chapultepec Park yesterday," said David. "Why are they doing it?" I asked. "The four men had to leap from the top of the pole thirteen times while others danced around them," explained Joseph. "The total of fifty two leaps represented the life span of the Sun God. Every fifty two years, major sacrifices had to be made to resurrect the Sun God."

Joseph gave us plenty of time to study all the paintings. As we left the National Palace and came back into the Zocalo, he told us, "The Zocalo was situated at the centre of the old city and was known as the Square of the Three Cultures, Aztec, Spanish and Modern." Pointing out a number of people standing by the railings at the side of the square, he added, "These are all tradesmen, painters, plumbers, builders and electricians, offering their services. If you live in Mexico City and need some work done, you come to the Zocalo to hire your labour."

Joseph then described the terrible earthquake in 1985. "It measured 8.6 on the Richter Scale," he said. "It was one of the most severe ever recorded. Nine hundred people were killed and many buildings collapsed. Those that remained standing were considered earthquake-proof but as you go around Mexico City, you will notice that many buildings lean at an angle."

National Palace
(Jahn Reinhard, Wikipedia Commons)

Part of Diego Rivera painting showing pole spinners

Basilica of the Virgin of Guadalupe

Palacio de Bellas Artes, Mexico City

Our next visit was to the Basilica of the Virgin of Guadalupe which was some distance away, so we returned to the coach. On the way there, Joseph told us the story of the Virgin. "In 1531, Juan Diego, an Indian who had recently been converted to Christianity, was standing on a hill, the Cerro del Tepeyac just outside Mexico City, when he saw a vision of the Virgin Mary dressed as an Indian princess. He rushed down the hill and told the local bishop, asking him to build a church in her honour. The bishop didn't believe his story and asked for proof. The following day, the Indian went back to the hill and saw the vision again. He returned to the bishop with a bunch of roses wrapped in his cloak, despite it being the middle of winter. When the roses were unwrapped, they left the imprint of a dark face and figure on the cloak so the bishop accepted his story and built the church."

"Over the years, the dark-skinned Virgin of Guadalupe was given the credit for many miracles which encouraged the population to convert to Christianity," Joseph continued. "Her fame spread across the country and eventually, after she had ended an outbreak of typhoid in 1737, she was declared the patron saint of Mexico. Although there are shrines to the Virgin across the country, the most revered is the one at the Cerro del Tepeyac, about four miles north of the Zocalo, and that is where we are going now. Pilgrims come here in their thousands from all over the country and beyond. The church was built over a shrine to Tonantzin who had been worshipped as the Mother Goddess by the Aztecs and, even today, descendants of the Aztecs still address the Virgin of Guadalupe as Tonantzin."

The coach was parked a short distance from the square in which the church was situated and we walked towards it along a narrow approach road. Set into the wall along the left side of this road was a series of shrines where worshippers were burning candles and praying. The right side of the street was lined with stalls selling candles, rosaries and also Indian charms and fetishes.

The square itself was large and contained some magnificent 16th century churches. Joseph pointed out the original Basilica, started in 1531, which had a large golden yellow central dome with a small golden yellow dome on each of its bell towers. The building was leaning at an angle, its left side much lower than its right side, and the red domed church to its right was leaning in a similar direction.

"Like the Cathedral, the original Basilica is sinking at an angle into the old lake bed", Joseph explained. "It was also too small to cope with the number of visiting pilgrims, particularly on the feast day of the patron saint, 12 December, when literally hundreds of thousands of worshippers arrive, some coming several days in advance. In the 1970s, a decision was taken to build a new Basilica next to the original church. It is supported on a pylon sunk deep into the ground to stabilise it."

The new Basilica of the Virgin of Guadalupe was in complete contrast to the lovely old Spanish churches. It was circular, the walls constructed in a light brown stone in two tiers, the upper level divided into decorative oblongs. A white cross in a light brown surround rose above the main entrance and a green copper roof curved gently up to a white airy structure of struts around the apex, topped with a futuristic light brown coronet above which rose another cross. The building looked elegant and modern.

As we walked towards it, Joseph told us, "During the feast day celebrations, this square is filled with music and dancing. Twenty thousand pilgrims arrive every single day to attend the forty services held in the various chapels of the Basilica but up to forty thousand can be accommodated at any one time. Many approach on their knees from a distance of more than three kilometres away although others will only fall to their knees from the far end of the square." Peter added, "After the Vatican City, the Basilica of the Virgin of Guadalupe is the most important shrine of Catholicism in the world, based on the number of visitors it receives."

Not far away, we saw a woman in her thirties dressed in a white blouse and black trousers inching forward on her knees, holding the hand of a young schoolgirl, probably her daughter, dressed in white blouse and black gymslip, white socks and black shoes, who was walking besides her holding a large bouquet of flowers. Her progress was very slow and she was clearly finding it extremely painful.

As we entered the Basilica, we found that a service was taking place in the main body of the church. The altar stood on a dais set back from the centre, the picture of the Virgin being visible on the wall behind. The pews in front of the altar radiated out in segments, with ushers directing people to the appropriate areas. We had to wait for a suitable break in the service and we were then permitted to go down a flight of steps behind the altar.

At the bottom was a moving walkway on which we were slowly carried past what was said to be the part of the original sisal cloak, nearly five hundred years old, imprinted with the picture of the Virgin. She was standing on a crescent moon, wearing a blue cloak edged in brown over a light gold dress and completely surrounded by a golden halo. This remarkably bright, sharp, well preserved picture was hung in a gold and gilt frame, on a wall where long golden blocks stood out proud from a background of dark red oblong blocks. We then travelled on another walkway, moving past the picture in the opposite direction, before leaving the Basilica.

We still had a lot to see that day so for lunch, Joseph took us a short distance to a café in another square. "To save time, I'll order tacos for us all," said Peter. "Is there anyone here who can't eat chicken?" There were no vegetarians or vegans in the group so Peter ordered a chicken taco for each of us. The tacos were a type of tortilla wrap, tasty and quick to eat, and within less than half an hour we were back in the coach and on our way again.

We now drove out of Mexico City into the country. On the outskirts of the city, the hillsides were covered with rapidly spreading shanty towns. "People are trying to escape the poverty of the countryside and they come flocking to the capital to find work and make their fortunes," said Joseph. "They are generally unskilled and many seek work in the building industry but it takes a long time to make any money. When a certain number have moved into a particular area, the Government will provide them with cheap water and electricity and the materials to build permanent accommodation but before constructing their homes, the inhabitants must first build schools, hospitals, clinics and shops." This sounded an excellent system.

"It is estimated that there are more than a hundred million Mexicans, including fifty nine different Indian tribes, sixty percent of whom are concentrated in cities with many emigrating to the USA," he continued. "All children are educated in primary school, where they use books printed in eight different languages. By the time the children reach secondary school, however, they are expected to be fluent in Spanish and all teaching is in that language."

We were now travelling through the fertile valley of Teotihuacán to the north east of Mexico City. Here we stopped at a plantation to learn about the many uses of the agave cactus, a large blue-green plant with very long fleshy leaves which was growing everywhere. We were taken round by the plantation guide, a dark-haired young woman in her early twenties.

"The outer leaf of the agave was used by the Aztecs and Mayans to make parchment and is very fine and strong," she told us. "It can also be split into a thread which takes dyes easily and can be woven or spun, while the tip of the leaf makes a needle." She gave each of us a length of cactus thread which was very much finer than cotton thread and more closely resembled dralon. It had the thickness, texture and appearance of grey hair and was quite difficult to break.

"The pulp of the leaf is used for making soap and shampoo," our guide continued, "and in the centre of the agave cactus is a sweet syrup which attracts bees and is used to make spirits such as tequila and mescal. A worm or grub, also from the cactus, is added to each bottle of mescal to enhance the flavour." "When you finish the mescal, you must eat the worm," Joseph added. The thought of it put me off completely.

At this point, we were each given a tiny plastic cup of tequila with a slice of lime and some salt on a saucer. "You must lick the back of your hand, dip it in the salt, lick the salt, suck the lime and drink the tequila to mix the flavours," Joseph grinned. "This is the margarita." We all tried it and it was all right but I thought that without the lime and salt, the tequila would have been rather tasteless and watery.

Still marvelling at the many uses of the agave cactus, we went into the souvenir shop where David and I bought a tablecloth made from agave thread and printed with an Aztec design. There were some beautiful hand cut obsidian sculptures but they cost a fortune, the ones I liked being priced at upwards of £1,000 each. Outside the shop, we had seen men seated along a bench beside a row of machines with which they were cutting the obsidian, their noses and mouths covered by scarves to protect their lungs from the dust. The machine-cut pieces were also on sale at prices we could afford but in comparison with the hand-cut designs, they looked crude, so we were not interested. While I was looking around, I put my camera down and nearly walked out of the shop without it, just remembering it in time.

It was not far from here to the Aztec ruins of Teotihuacán. These were on a long narrow site with a parking area at either end and one near the centre. The coach parked near the centre and we entered the site along a road leading to the huge Pyramid of the Sun. The left side of this approach road was lined with souvenir stalls. The sky had clouded over during the afternoon and the pyramid in front of us was silhouetted against a black cloud which made it look quite dramatic.

"That sounds like gunfire," said Ian looking concerned. Around us, we could hear loud bangs and explosions. "Are we safe in this area?" asked Diane. "Don't worry," Joseph reassured us. "It's just the farmers setting off rockets to scare away the Rain God and protect their prickly pear cactus crops." Kayleigh giggled. "Hey, that's neat," she grinned and we all agreed with her.

Once we had entered the site, we stopped while Joseph gave us his tourist guide talk. "Teotihuacán was once the capital city of the Aztecs and is much older than the ruins of Tenochtitlán that you saw earlier today. Construction began in the 1st century AD and the city was erected without the aid of any machinery or pack animals. One of the first buildings to be completed was the magnificent Pyramid of the Sun. This was positioned on the site of an older altar to the Sun God, dating from 200 BC, because it was from here that the Aztecs believed life originated. It is more than 220 metres square and about 70 metres high, making it the third largest pyramid in the world, exceeded in size only by the Egyptian pyramids of the pharaohs Khufu and Khafre." "I think they are the same as Cheops and Chephren," Neville whispered to Diane.

"At one time, there would have been a temple on the top, making it even higher," continued Joseph. "This pyramid set the orientation for the entire city and at a certain time of the year, the sun's rays fell vertically over the centre of the temple on top. The upper levels were originally covered in limestone plaster, decorated with brightly coloured fresco designs. The background was painted a vivid red which would have glowed in the evening sun."

The pyramid was built in six tiers, the vertical wall of the bottom tier creating a base platform, while all the other tiers sloped inwards. Facing us, steps led up the centre of the first, third, fifth and sixth tiers of the pyramid, very wide at the base and narrowing towards the top. The second tier had three sub-tiers up the centre with a flight of steps on either side and the fourth tier also had two flights of steps, on either side of a central panel. At the top was a platform where once the temple would have stood.

While the Egyptian pyramids were built with large limestone or granite blocks, some weighing fifteen tons or more, the Pyramid of the Sun was constructed from comparatively small stones and pebbles. These ranged in colour from deep red-brown to pink and creamy orange-yellow and from blue-black to grey and sparkling white. Their shapes and sizes were equally varied. At the lower levels, which had not been covered over by limestone plaster, the stones were meant to be seen and admired. The surface was almost flat and each stone was set in mortar and surrounded by a row of tiny black pebbles, separating it from its neighbours. The overall effect at a distance was of an uneven colour wash of cream and brown but seen close-up, the stones were beautiful.

We climbed to the top of the pyramid from where there was an excellent view of the smaller Pyramid of the Moon to our right, at the northern end of a road known as the Avenue of the Dead. Below us was the Plaza of the Sun and the sacrificial altar. The site was surrounded by hills.

So far, the rockets had been successful in scaring away the rain and the dark clouds were beginning to retreat. We descended the pyramid and Joseph took us along the Avenue of the Dead to the Pyramid of the Moon. Although this was a smaller pyramid, it was constructed on higher ground so its summit was at about the same height as that of the Pyramid of the Sun. The Pyramid of the Moon was designed differently, with a flight of about forty steps, leading up to a platform built forward from the main pyramid. Behind the platform, the pyramid continued upwards with two additional sloping tiers, each cut by a central flight of steps, and with a more rounded top.

In front of the Pyramid of the Moon was a large open plaza, in the centre of which stood a raised square platform with a flight of about seven steps up the centre of each side. "Was that the sacrificial altar?" I asked. "No," said Joseph. "This platform is thought to have been used for religious dancing. All the sacrifices were made in front of the Temple of the Sun God."

Joseph decided to tell us more about the sacrifices. "It was an honour to be selected for sacrifice and not something to be feared," he said. "The victim was drugged, so he was relaxed and happy. He would lie back comfortably against a backrest and his arms and legs would be held by priests while the high priest cut right across under his ribs with a sharp obsidian knife. He would then reach inside and draw out the heart, still beating, cutting the blood vessels." At this point, Kayleigh and Lynn looked quite ill but Joseph continued.

"The heart would be placed in a sacred bowl and left in the open to be taken to the gods by a bird of prey such as an eagle or hawk. Usually, victims were sacrificed one at a time; remember the man in the sedan chair in the Diego Rivera picture this morning? However, for the dedication of Tenochtitlán's great temple in 1487, the Aztec emperor Ahuizotl sacrificed twenty thousand captives. When you were in the Anthropological Museum yesterday, you would have seen the sacred bowl into which all their hearts were placed." I recalled seeing the bowl which had seemed far too small to hold a hundred hearts, let alone twenty thousand.

"Similar numbers were sacrificed every fifty two years, which was considered to be the end of the Sun's lifespan," Joseph continued. "This would renew the Sun's life for a further fifty two years. The Aztecs believed that four previous worlds had been destroyed by the death of the Sun, wiping out humanity. They were living on the fifth world." This failed to explain how the Sun had come back to life and a new world had been created each time the Sun had died but I assumed that there would be legends to cover this.

Around the Moon Plaza were twelve platforms, each four tiers high with a central flight of steps to the top, which Joseph told us had been used for astrological purposes. He then took us to a building on the right side of the Moon Plaza when facing down the Avenue of the Dead. "This is the Palace of the Quetzalpapalotl or Quetzal Butterfly," he said. "It is thought to have been the home of someone of importance, possibly a king or high priest."

The Palace was built on a platform at the top of a wide flight of steps and had a flat roof with deep edges supported by square pillars. The sides of the roof and the interior walls were decorated like the base layer of the Sun Pyramid, with coloured stones set in mortar, each separated from its neighbours by a line of tiny black pebbles.

We climbed the steps and entered the portico where a guide was explaining a mural to a large party of visitors. After waiting a while for them to move on, Joseph beckoned us to follow him and we passed them and went out into a small patio. The flat roof over the building surrounding the courtyard was supported by square pillars. On the roof above each of the pillars stood a stone merlon, shaped a little like the top half of a Celtic cross but decorated with a circle in the centre, capped by a double inverted V in the widening top section. Round the deep edge of the roof was a plaster-covered frieze painted red, with a stencilled row of white circles along the top and bottom edges and a formal, oblong shaped repeat design in the inset area between.

The square pillars were constructed of square and oblong bricks of different sizes, fitted perfectly together, before being carved and painted. Joseph pointed out the designs representing the hybrid of a quetzal bird and butterfly. Facing into the courtyard was a side view with the head feathers swept backwards while the sides of the pillars gave a front view with the head feathers upright. The beak of the bird in both perspectives curved downwards and the eyes were of black obsidian. The carvings were still sharp and pastel tinted in red, blue, orange-brown, grey and white.

Pyramid of the Sun, Teotihuacán

Pyramid of the Moon from the Pyramid of the Sun

Part of the Pyramid of Quetzalcoatl

Detail of Jaguar head

Joseph then led us behind and below this building into the basement of the adjacent Jaguar Palace. It was dark and we needed the torches which we had been asked to bring along with us, but the lack of light meant that there were some well preserved murals. Joseph showed us one painted in green, white and pink on a red background. "This shows the Jaguar God in a feathered headdress, blowing into a conch shell and praying to the Rain God, Tlaloc," he explained. Along the top of the mural was a frieze of alternate feathered headdresses and white circles, each circle containing a five-pointed star standing on two short legs with large feet and with a red face in the centre of the star, its round ears, eyes and straight mouth all outlined in white. "Those look like something from a child's cartoon," chuckled Cheryl. "Each of those large circles portrays Tlaloc," remonstrated Joseph, but with a smile. "The star shape represents the feathers round his head."

From the Jaguar Palace, a narrow underground passage took us into the Temple of the Plumed Conch Shells. Here we saw engravings of large shells decorated with feathers and four-petalled flowers, similar to Tudor roses. Below these was a mural which was not very clear. However, opposite the exit door, a portion of the mural could be seen in daylight. It was crudely drawn but showed a large bird with a yellow eye surrounded by red, a red breast and a yellow beak, from which water gushed on to what might possibly have been a yellow fledgling in its nest with its wings spread. Below the stream of water stood a row of what appeared to be red flasks outlined in black, presumably lined up to catch the water, but it was very difficult to tell.

From here we made our way back to the Moon Plaza. "It's a long way to the other end of the site so we'll go there on the coach," said Joseph. As we walked down the Avenue of the Dead, Lynn asked, "Did this road get its name from the sacrifices at the Pyramid of the Sun?" "Actually, no," said Joseph. "The road was once lined with pyramids that included important civic buildings as well as temples. At some stage, the city was abandoned but later Aztecs still revered it as a sacred site of the Sun God and the origin of life and they came here on pilgrimages. They thought that all the pyramids were tombs, either of early Aztec kings or of gods, who had sacrificed themselves to bring life back to the Sun God at the beginning of the fifth world. This is why the Aztecs called it the Avenue of the Dead and knew the city as The Place of the Gods."

We travelled about a kilometre by coach to the parking area near the south end of the site, saving us time and energy. The road from the coach park was again lined with souvenir stalls but Joseph was hurrying on ahead and we had no time to stop and look. At the end of the road near the Avenue of the Dead was a museum, but we went straight past this and crossed a wide grassed area to the Pyramid of Quetzalcoatl, the feathered serpent.

The sky was still overcast although less dark and stormy looking than it had been earlier. The rockets were still being fired every few seconds and we hoped that the farmers would continue to be successful at scaring away the rain. As we came into the temple area, we found that it was very different in design from the pyramids we had already seen. On either side of the steps leading up the centre was a sloping parapet on which, at regular intervals, sat heads of the feathered serpent, Quetzalcoatl. The feathers were like the petals of an enormous flower against the parapet with the head of the serpent, its teeth viciously bared, protruding from the centre.

On the far side of each parapet were deep stepped tiers, each about ten feet high. The vertical walls of each tier were divided by a projecting row of stones about a third of the way up. The lower section was carved into what appeared to be stylistic waves with shells in the spaces between the curves. The upper section also had a background of waves and shells, superimposed with snarling feathered heads jutting out from the wall. Between these was a design of four circles in a background of small squares that I imagined to be scales, with a protruding line of small squares under the circles, that could have been a mouth.

"The wavy lines represent the bodies of the serpents on the parapets," explained Joseph. "There is some doubt about the heads with the four circles. Some think that this is the symbol of Tlaloc the Rain God while others think it represents the Fire Serpent, who was the Bearer of the Sun on its daily journey across the sky. The four circles are his eyes and were once filled with pieces of obsidian. The heads surrounded by plumes of feathers on either side of the parapets represent either more serpents or jaguars, which are the symbol of the God of Thunder. You can also see seashells, including conch shells, incorporated in the background design. There were originally seven carved facades, one above the other but, as you can see, only four now remain. The designs would once have been painted in vivid colours and the temple is believed to date back to about 250-300 AD."

There was still some residual pastel colouring in the carvings. The waves were a variety of colours but the shells were pink, the feathered heads were blue with white teeth surrounded by pink petal-feathers and the heads of circles and small squares were blue and yellow. When the colours were bright and fresh, the design would have been outstanding.

The temple was situated in a large square complex at the far end of the Avenue of the Dead. "This area was known as La Ciudadela or the Citadel," said Joseph. "It once had four wide walls, each three hundred and ninety metres long, topped by fifteen pyramids which probably included the Royal Palace and residences of the priests and government officials. This would have been the administrative centre of the city, in the very heart of Teotihuacán. From here, the Avenue of the Dead extended for about two kilometres in either direction with another major avenue crossing it at right angles, dividing the city into four quarters. The Citadel would have held thousands of people for religious ceremonies and the remains of sacrificial victims have been discovered on either side of the Pyramid of Quetzalcoatl."

"At its peak," Joseph went on, "Teotihuacán was Mexico's largest ancient city with a population of about two hundred thousand people. It controlled an empire which covered most of Mexico, Guatemala, Belize and parts of Honduras and El Salvador. Literacy was widespread throughout most of this empire and the Aztecs would have used the Mayan writing system which had between three hundred and five hundred symbols, plus a bar and dot numerical system." He added, "The Aztecs also had a calendar, but counted time in various ways. They used almanac years consisting of thirteen periods of twenty days and solar years made up of eighteen months of twenty days with a five day period between years. They also measured time in units of twenty, three hundred and sixty, seven thousand two hundred and one hundred and forty four thousand days." This all sounded very confusing.

Our tour was now over and Joseph led us back to the coach just as it began to spot with rain. No sooner were we all inside than the rockets finally lost the fight with Tlaloc and the skies let loose a tropical downpour. We counted ourselves very fortunate to have completed our tour in the dry.

On the way back to the hotel, Peter warned us that the next day, we would have a six hour drive to our destination. "We won't be arriving until early afternoon, so you'll need to stock up on food and drink for lunch on the journey," he said. "If you turn right out of the hotel, you'll find a supermarket a short distance away."

As we got off the coach, we thanked Joseph for all the fascinating information he had given us over the past two days. David and I then went up to our room, collected our waterproofs and went straight out again into the rain to do our shopping. The supermarket was three blocks away and we met several of our friends inside. We walked round first to see what was available, made our purchases and took them back to our hotel room. Having hung our wet clothes out to dry, we then did most of the packing and wrote a few postcards.

By the time we met up with the group in the lobby at 7.30 pm, the rain had stopped, although David and I had brought our waterproofs with us to be on the safe side. As we left the hotel, Peter said, "We shall have to walk quickly this evening. I'm heading for the Latin American Tower which is forty four floors high with a wonderful view from the top, but it's quite a long way. If you want to go up, you need to be there before it gets dark. After that, you're free to spend the rest of the evening as you wish." He turned to the right along the Paseo de la Reforma and then right again down the Avenida Juarez in the direction of the old town and the Zocalo. Election bunting was strung across both these roads.

On the way he told us, "Air pollution is a problem here because warm air from the valley is trapped by the surrounding mountains.

There's also a shortage of oxygen because of the altitude. There are nearly five million cars in use in and around the city, many very old and poorly maintained, so the Government has brought in a scheme whereby cars have been issued with different coloured number plates. Every car is banned from entering the city one day a week, depending on the colour of its number plate. There's a fine of $800 for bringing your car in on a prohibited day." It sounded an excellent idea although people travelling a distance into the city to work each day would probably either have to join a car-sharing scheme or stagger their working week.

Twenty minutes of fast walking brought us to the Palacio de Bellas Artes, a magnificent concert hall and art centre. This building was a medley of classical pillars and arches with a central segmented dome topped by an angel. "If you turn down this street to the left," said Peter, pointing out the road on the far side of the building, "you'll come to an area famous for its mariachi bands. There will usually be a trumpeter, a guitarist and possibly a violinist, with a singer dressed up as a Mexican cowboy. If you pay them some money, they'll play for you." "That sounds good," Lynn said to Alan. "I wouldn't mind doing that later." "We'll come with you," said Cheryl.

From here, we could see the square skyscraper of the Latin American Tower, its two smaller observation floors at the top supporting a tall column with a mast. Although the light was beginning to fade by the time we arrived, most of us decided to go up the tower and queued for our tickets. A large lift holding about twenty people took us up to the thirty seventh floor. We then transferred to a smaller lift which held only six of us at a time and took us to the forty second floor.

From here we climbed stairs to a glass-encased look-out platform and took photographs across the city. More stairs took us to the top of the tower where the view was only obscured by open wire mesh. The holes were large enough to poke the lens of a camera through, which was even better for photographs. There seemed to be very little pollution and we could see for miles across the city to the hills beyond. The views were wonderful and we stayed up there until dusk fell and we were able to watch the city lighting up.

As the group gradually dispersed, Neville asked us, "Have you any plans for this evening? Kayleigh's gone off with the Australian youngsters to hear the mariachi bands but we didn't feel like another long walk to get there." "We thought we'd go to the 'House of Tiles' for a meal," said David. "Peter recommended it and according to the map it isn't far away. Would you like to join us?" "That's very kind of you," smiled Diane. "We'd love to but you must let us buy the wine. By the way, did you see Sonia this evening?" "No," I said. "I should imagine she stayed behind to ring the hospital again about her father. She's really worried about him."

We had a lovely meal, each ordering a different item from the menu. I decided to try chicken with mole, a chocolate sauce flavoured with ground up chilli peppers and spices, described as a typical Aztec dish. When I ordered, I asked the waiter if it was possible to have the sauce not too hot and I thoroughly enjoyed my meal although chicken and chocolate was not a combination I would normally have considered. David and Diane both tasted it and although David was not too keen, Diane definitely approved.

By the time we were ready to leave, it was pouring with rain again. After about ten minutes, we managed to flag down a taxi but found it would only seat two. "You and Neville take it," I said to Diane, because the two of them had no protection from the rain. "David and I are both wearing waterproofs so we can walk."

We waved to them as they were driven away and started back to the hotel. After our large meal, we were actually quite glad to have some exercise before going to bed and we arrived back just before midnight.

Tuesday 1st July

The next morning, I looked out of our bedroom window at 6 am to see a thick mantle of yellow-grey dust everywhere. "Come and look at this," I said to David. "Do you think it's sand blown in from the desert?" He came over to look. Cleaners were already hard at work with their brooms, sweeping it off the roads and pavements into piles at the side of the street but there was still a thick coating over everything else. "I suppose it could be," he said, doubtfully. "The desert isn't very far to the north but when sand blows in from the Sahara in England, there's usually only a very fine covering of dust."

We were leaving that morning so we finished the last of the packing, took our cases down to the lobby and went in for breakfast. Peter was already in the restaurant, collecting his food from the buffet. "Did you see that dust outside?" he asked. "Yes," said David. "We were wondering where it came from." "It's nothing to worry about," Peter assured us, "but the nearby volcano, Popocatapetl, has been erupting ash for most of the night and the city has been put on yellow alert. If it reaches the next stage, a red alert, the entire city will have to be evacuated." "How exciting," I said, "but does that mean we'll have problems with traffic congestion?" "No," said Peter. "Everybody ignores a yellow alert. Even so, I'd like to set off promptly by eight o'clock."

He passed the word on to the rest of the group and before the given time, all the luggage had been loaded and we were on board the coach and ready to leave. "You may have noticed that Sonia is no longer with us," said Peter as he finished counting heads. "She decided yesterday afternoon that she had to return home and after I left you at the Latin American Tower, I went with her to the airport to see her through check-in. Luckily she got away before the volcano started erupting. Once the ash started falling, the airport was closed for several hours."

As we made our way out of Mexico City, he told us that the ash made the runways very slippery and there was also a danger that ash could get into the engines and cause them to fail. "Later on, once the severity of the eruption had been assessed, about 40% of flights managed to take off and land but the runways and the wheels of the planes had to be washed clean of ash between flights." He added, "Popocatapetl is an Aztec name meaning 'smoking mountain'. We'll pass it on our way to Oaxaca. If you're very lucky, you may be able to see the eruption."

Our route took us past the foot of the volcano but Popocatapetl is more than 17,500 feet high and not surprisingly, most of it was hidden by low cloud. We noticed that houses had been built all over the lower slopes which seemed extremely risky to say the least.

The scenery on our journey was very varied, taking us through lush green areas and arid sandy regions, over mountain passes and across flat plains. At about 11 am, we had a break at a roadside petrol station and café to use the toilets, have a drink and give the driver a short break. We also had a brief stop to look at some cacti that had spread across the hillsides like a forest of bare upright poles with segmented stems, some slightly bent over and with a lighter colour at the top of the stalk. "Although they look bare at the moment, these cacti do flower and spread by seeding," Peter told us.

Just after midday, David and I unwrapped our picnic lunch from the supermarket and ate it on the coach which made the rest of the journey pass very quickly. By 2.30 pm, we were coming into the city of Oaxaca, where we were spending the next two nights.

2

Oaxaca, the Zapotecs and the Mixtecs

As we drove towards the city centre Peter told us, "Oaxaca stands fifteen hundred metres above sea level and was built by the Spaniards in 1530, on the site of an Aztec settlement called Huaxyacac, meaning 'Place of the Gourds'. We are still in an earthquake zone which is the reason why few buildings here are more than two storeys high."

Our hotel was in a wonderful position on a corner of the zocalo, the main square, which was well shaded by trees in the centre and covered arcades around the outside. We were free for the rest of the afternoon and as soon as our rooms had been allocated and Peter had given each of us a hand-drawn map of the city centre, David and I went off to explore. By now, I had written quite a few postcards, so our first task was to find the Post Office which was situated on Independencia, a street just off the zocalo on the far side of the cathedral. We queued up, bought some stamps, posted our cards and then went to a nearby money exchange kiosk to top up our supply of Mexican pesos.

As we were still near the zocalo, our next visit was to the cathedral, a beautiful old building in honey-coloured stone with a bell tower on either side. Between the bell towers, the frontage was divided into three tiers and there were three entrance portals. On either side of the central arch, the statue of a saint stood in a niche flanked by columns and this design was repeated in the two tiers above, the saints in the upper tiers being separated by central decorative panels above the arch. The smaller arches on either side were each set back in a recess with figures carved into the upper tiers above them. In the centre of the roof rose a curved façade with statues on either side. Floodlights were attached to nearby lampposts to illuminate the cathedral after dark.

Outside on the zocalo stood balloon sellers with enormous bunches of brightly coloured helium-filled balloons floating on strings above their heads, and with dozens of blow-up plastic animals and twisted balloon animals in all colours, shapes and sizes around their feet. It looked very picturesque.

We entered the cathedral and were quite shocked. Instead of the quiet religious atmosphere we were expecting, we found that the locals were using the building as a place to sleep, have lunch and trade goods. It seemed very sacrilegious. Just as we were about to leave, it began to rain and some of the balloon sellers came rushing inside with their bunches of helium balloons while others stood and sheltered under the covered colonnades around the square.

While we waited for the rain to stop, David asked, "Where would you like to go next? Let's have a look at the map." "I thought we could visit the Benito Juarez Market," I suggested, pointing it out to him. "It's only three blocks away." The shower was only brief and as the sun came out again, the balloon sellers left the cathedral and we followed them out. The market was just a few minutes walk away to the south of the cathedral and was a fascinating place.

Some women stood outside the market hall selling bowls of black stick-like insects with an accompaniment of red chillies. "Excuse me, what are those?" I asked. "Chapulines," was the reply. We were none the wiser until one of their customers explained. "They are a local speciality, fried grasshoppers. Try one," and she held out the paper bag containing some she had just purchased. We were not feeling brave enough at the time. "That's very kind of you but we've just eaten," said David, thanking her with a smile.

"Would you tell me what that is, please?" I asked her before she went. A nearby stall had earthenware pots along the front containing something that was pale yellow and looked solid while on the stall stood a row of spherical objects in the same colour, slightly larger than tennis balls and wrapped in cellophane. "That's cheese," she told us. As we ventured further into the market, we found another stall where a woman was rolling the balls from long narrow flat strips of cheese. The balls of cheese were then covered in cellophane to keep them clean and stop them drying out.

There were all kinds of fresh, healthy-looking fruits, vegetables, herbs and spices. Less healthy-looking were the fish, meat and sausages which were covered in flies, despite the efforts of the stallholders to fan them away. There were some beautiful leather goods, particularly handbags and leather belts partly covered in a woven fabric; black glazed pottery; very brightly painted angular animals and sinuous snakes made of wood; and decorations in foil and tinsel.

From here we went to the Artisan's Market. We expected this to sell a variety of handicrafts but in comparison with Benito Juarez Market, we found it a little disappointing as it contained only fabrics. However, we saw some colourful woven blankets and beautifully embroidered blouses and waistcoats.

The markets were closing for the evening by the time we left and we returned to the hotel for a refreshing shower before the evening meal. When we met up with the others, Peter said, "I know of a good restaurant, only five minutes away, but you'll need your waterproofs." As we left the hotel, the rain was lashing down. There were no drain holes in the road and streets swiftly turned into rivers. As we walked past the cathedral, drainpipes gushed out water at us across the pavement and we were soon drenched.

We decided it had been worth the soaking when we arrived at a lovely restaurant with atmosphere, live music and good food. I tried a local speciality called tamales, a type of steamed dumpling. My first tamale turned out to be stuffed with chicken and mole, a little similar to the meal I had had the previous evening. Peter told me that as well as chocolate, the black mole sauce was made from thirty five different spices which, at this restaurant, did not include chillies. My second tamale was sweet, slightly stodgy and wrapped in a banana leaf. It was an acquired taste but once I had become accustomed to it, quite enjoyable and very filling.

During the meal, the rain stopped and the water in the street subsided. To complete the evening, we stopped to listen to a mariachi band on the way back to the hotel.

Wednesday 2nd July

The next morning, we met in the lobby at 8am after an excellent breakfast of muesli, fresh fruit salad and scrambled eggs. As we set off in the coach, Peter told us, "This morning, we are going to visit the Zapotec site at Monte Alban. This dates back to about 400 BC, far older than anything you have already seen."

The ancient city had been built on top of a hill, four hundred metres higher than the surrounding countryside and two thousand metres above sea level. As our coach began to climb, we were soon enveloped in low misty cloud which gradually thickened. When we arrived at the site, Peter took us to the entrance where we met our guide, Ernesto, a large man in his early forties with twinkling blue eyes under thick bushy eyebrows, untidy long black hair and beard and an infectious enthusiasm for the site which he clearly loved.

He led us up the hillside in thick fog to what he told us was the highest point and assured us that the cloud would soon blow over. Then, as we stood in a steady drizzle, he told us that we were located at the very heart of the Americas and that all trade between North and South America had passed through Monte Alban.

"The city was founded by the Zapotecs some time between 800 and 400 BC," Ernesto informed us. "At its peak, between 300 and 700 AD, the population of Monte Alban reached about twenty five thousand and the slopes of all the surrounding hills were terraced with living accommodation. Surprisingly, although the Zapotecs had discovered the wheel nearly two thousand years ago and had learnt how to mix gold and silver, they had no metal tools and all their buildings were constructed by hand, using one rock to shape another. They were skilled astronomers and each of the buildings on the centre hill is

46

lined up to a different planet. Many of these buildings would have been plastered and painted red, the colour of life and power."

While our guide was speaking to us, the clouds gradually began to lift and we could make out the nearest part of the city which, according to Ernesto, once covered a total area of twenty square kilometres. "We are now on the North Platform," he said, "and on a clear day, it's possible to see as far as the Pacific coast." From the hill on which we stood, we were looking down on a small, flat, grassy square plaza surrounded by stone walls and steps and with a square raised platform in the centre. Through the thinning mist, we could now make out the hazy outlines of further buildings beyond the plaza.

Ernesto led us to the rim of the small plaza and then down a wide, steep flight of steps to the flat grassy area. The surrounding walls were partly vertical and partly sloping, made of stones set in concrete. "You are now standing in the Sunken Patio," he told us. "The raised area in the centre was an altar and on either side of the main staircase, we have discovered chambers containing tombs. Some of these were decorated with frescoes and would have been for men of importance."

We made our way to the altar and then turned left to the main staircase. This consisted of an even wider flight of steps, at the top of which was a broad platform. On this stood the remains of twelve pillars arranged in two rows. "At one time, these twelve columns supported the roof of a great hall," said Ernesto. "On the other side of the platform is the Grand Plaza, the centre of Monte Alban."

Although the mist was still drifting across, it was rapidly clearing. We climbed the steps and from the platform of the Great Hall, Ernesto pointed out the main buildings below us. "At the far end of the Grand Plaza is the South Platform," he said. "To the left are the Ball Court, a small temple, the high priest's accommodation with a square altar in front of it and the Royal Palace. At the far end is the Observatory, which stands at an angle of 45° to all the other Grand Plaza buildings. Inside, it is riddled with tunnels and staircases. On the right of the Grand Plaza are a further temple and other civic buildings."

We descended into the Grand Plaza and as Ernesto took us around the site, he told us, "The Zapotecs used two calendars, one for the Sun and one for the Moon, that interlocked like the cogs of a wheel. Both calendars completed a circuit every 52 years. The Zapotecs calculated the exact dates of the solstices and used holes and mirrors to reflect the rays of the Sun at these times. They knew all about the paths taken by each planet and foretold earthquakes and eclipses of the Sun, even to the most recent ones today."

"They have prophesied," he warned us, "that in the year 2013, all the planets will be aligned and there will be major catastrophes, climatic changes and severe earthquakes. The whole planet will be plunged into darkness, then light, then darkness again." We were very sceptical but Ernesto was so serious that we wondered if there might be something in it.

In the centre of the Plaza was a very high platform. This had a broad flight of steps taking up most of the side facing the high priest's house and the altar, which was square and stood in the centre of the grassed area in between. The platform steps served the same purpose as seats at a theatre.

"When a solstice was due," Ernesto informed us, "all the dignitaries of the city would be seated on the steps facing the altar and the sacrificial victim, who would be there waiting. At just the right moment, the high priest, clothed in a magnificent ceremonial costume of gold, silver, pearls and jade, would take an underground tunnel from his house and would leap out on to the altar at the very instant that the rays of the Sun reflected through a hole, off a mirror, and then directly on to him, so that he glowed like a god and all the onlookers would be filled with awe." As he was speaking, he was pointing out where everything was happening, bringing it vividly to life in our imaginations.

As we continued around the site, Ernesto showed us various plants that were used for dyes, food flavourings or for medicinal purposes.

Oaxaca

Observatory, Monte Alban

Danzante

Woman giving birth

Monte Alban Ball Court

To one side stood a row of stone tablets depicting figures in various poses, carved in relief upon the rock. "These are the Danzantes or dancers," said Ernesto. "The figures have thick lips and wide noses, similar to the statues of the Olmecs who probably originated from Africa." When I first heard the term 'Danzantes," I had visualised young, slim female dancers but the bas-relief figures on these particular stone stelae all looked like broad, thick-set, middle aged males with down-turned mouths and grim expressions and were presumably given the name because their arms and legs were at unusual angles.

Some of these stelae also bore hieroglyphs or dates in a dot and bar style. "The first Olmecs flourished from 1200 BC and used hieroglyphs and a dot and bar method of counting," said Ernesto. "They also invented a calendar and it is probable that they had a strong influence on the Zapotec culture."

Ernesto now moved on to some stone tablets that, he told us, indicated some medical knowledge, although it was not obvious to us. He then told us, "Remains found in the burial chambers show that men had had gold inserted in their skulls and the bone had grown back over the insertion. This proves that they continued to live after an operation which involved drilling into the brain."

Ernesto pointed out a tablet showing a pregnant woman giving birth. Between her legs were what appeared to be a pair of boots and socks while the head of the 'baby', still in the woman's belly, looked as though it had a beard and was wearing a hat. "If a baby or young child died," Ernesto informed us, "the infant would be left in the open until an animal approached the body. That animal then became the protector of the dead child. The child's remains would be put into a clay urn with the image of the protector animal engraved on the outside and the urn would be placed in a burial chamber."

Further on, we saw a tablet where the profile of the head appeared to show a worm or snake issuing vertically from the mouth. "This symbol indicates that the person is singing and is happy," said our guide. "In the National Museum in Mexico City, there is a fresco depicting Heaven where everyone is shown singing in this way, surrounded by abundant food and water."

After our tour with Ernesto finished, we were given nearly an hour to wander around by ourselves and soak up the atmosphere.IThe clouds were still covering the tops of the surrounding hills and it was grey and overcast but it was no longer drizzling with rain and we could see clearly across the site.

The group split up and wandered off in various directions. David and I went for another look at the Ball Court, a sunken rectangular area with vertical walls about four metres high and steps leading down from either end. Taking up more than half the length of each of the long sides and jutting in towards the centre was a sloping structure that may have provided a viewing area for spectators. This gave the area in which the game took place the approximate shape of a capital I. In two opposite corners of the court, there was a small vertical opening, about a metre high and about a third of a metre across.

"Players were not allowed to touch the ball with their hands or feet, only with knees, hips and elbows, which were covered for protection," Ernesto had explained to us. "In Monte Alban, the aim was to direct the ball into one of the vertical openings at either end of the court but in some places, the players had to make the ball pass through a ring standing out vertically from the wall. The first player to succeed had the honour of being sacrificed." "I should imagine nobody tried very hard to score," Sue had commented. "On the contrary," Ernesto had assured us. "Every player strived his utmost to achieve this honour so that he could go to Heaven where everyone was always singing and happy."

From here, we walked round to the altar and the steps from which the dignitaries would view the sacrifice. The Zapotecs of Monte Alban, like the Aztecs, cut out the hearts of their victims while they were still alive. In other areas, Ernesto had explained, different methods of sacrifice were preferred. In Yucatan, which suffered from water shortages, victims were thrown into a well to guarantee the water supply. I privately thought that the decaying bodies would have done little to improve the quality of the water. A third method, we were told, was to place the victim in a net which was slowly twisted until the body snapped – and people actually wanted to die like this!

Across the Grand Plaza was the Observatory. This was an unusual building where the walls, instead of being at right angles to each other, were all at different angles to the adjacent walls. They were also at different angles to the ground, one wall being vertical, another gently sloping and a third at an angle of 45°. On one side was a low wall, a grassed level area and then a single high wall while on another side, the wall was divided into three sections almost equal in height. A stone construction stood on the flat top of the Observatory. Ernesto had told us that all the tunnels and entrances within the Observatory were aligned to the paths taken by different planets and stars.

Before we left, Ernesto told us, "Monte Alban declined suddenly as a settlement and by 750 AD it was nearly deserted. Mixtecs began to arrive in this area from about 1100 AD and the tombs of Mixtec dignitaries have been found on Monte Alban. However, some Zapotecs remained in the area and today, there are about 500,000 Zapotecs, many of whom are farmers. The most famous Zapotec was probably Benito Juarez, a lawyer from Oaxaca who became a State Governor, known for reducing bureaucracy and opening new village schools. In 1861, he became President of Mexico and was responsible for widespread economic and educational reform." "There's a market in Oaxaca named after him," said Garry. "Yes, we were there yesterday," I said. "It's worth a visit."

After a fascinating morning, we rejoined the coach and returned to Oaxaca for lunch, which we had as a group in a restaurant in the zocalo. We were then free for the rest of the afternoon.

David and I decided to head in the opposite direction from the markets we had seen the previous day. One block north and one block east of the zocalo, we came to the Calle Alcala, a wide road of brown cobblestones, divided by two rows of lighter paving stones into three lanes. On the pavements on either side were antique-looking lampposts, each with three upright smoked glass lampshades in a wrought iron framework, two being set at a lower level on either end of a crossbar. The two-storey buildings were in honey-coloured stone with black wrought-iron balconies above the front doors.

Here we found the Museum of Contemporary Art. Above the doorway leading on to the museum's first floor balcony was a carved angel in an alcove with a shield on either side. As we were looking at it, one of the locals came up to us. "The museum is worth a visit," he encouraged us. "Shall we go in?" I asked. David was in an exploring mood. "Let's leave it until later and see some more of the town first."

We continued up the Calle Alcala. Further on, there was a barrier across the road in the form of a pair of low, black wrought iron gates which could be opened when required. At this point, the character of the buildings changed. We were now walking past single storey buildings, the walls of which had been plastered over and painted in warm attractive hues, one being emerald green, the next a light orange-brown, the following one a blue-grey. They had tall narrow stone-mullioned windows covered in black wrought iron grilles and the effect was very attractive. There seemed no reason why this should have been made a traffic-free zone as most people still kept to the pavements and we had, in any case, seen very little traffic in Oaxaca.

Then, above the buildings on the right, we saw the twin towers of a church. Our map told us that this was Santo Domingo Church, dating back to 1550 AD and one of the sights recommended by Peter as being worth a visit. Before we reached the church, David said, "I can hear music. Let's go and take a look." We turned right into a small square. A live band was playing in the centre of the square, valiantly competing against a group of Indians playing CDs of Mexican music which they were selling on a nearby stall.

Round the edge of the square was an open-air art exhibition. "Let's have a look at the paintings," I suggested. Although these were mainly abstract, brightly coloured and not to our taste, many of them were very skilfully composed.

We continued to the church, only to find that it was closed until 2.30 pm. Beside it was the Regional Museum of Oaxaca, situated in and around the cloisters of the church. The entrance fee was quite expensive and we were very disappointed to be told that only one room was open. "I'm sorry," said the woman at the ticket office, "but the rest of the museum and the cloisters are closed for renovation work." "Shall we forget it?" said David. "This is another place that Peter suggested we should see," I said. "We're here now and the church isn't open yet so we might as well go inside." We bought our tickets and entered a very dark room, illuminated only by the lights in the display cases.

That one room alone proved well worth the visit. The Mixtecs dominated the Oaxaca area in the 13th century and were noted for their pottery, metalwork and jewellery. In the museum, we saw some fabulous Mixtec relics including some very fine gold filigree jewellery, jade, carved jaguar teeth and bones and some amazing golden statuettes, including seated figures wearing feathered headdresses. Unfortunately, photography was forbidden.

When we were back outside, David saw a row of boot boys. "I'm going to have my shoes cleaned. They're very dusty," he said. "They'll get dusty again as you walk round the town." "It doesn't matter. I'm still having them cleaned." One of the boot boys beckoned David into a high leather chair and selected some black polish. This he rubbed in thickly and carefully with one of his brushes and then polished the shoes with two more brushes. The resulting shine was brilliant, far better than we would normally achieve at home. "You've done a good job," said David giving the young man a tip and he beamed.

By this time, Santo Domingo Church was open and we went inside. This was once the church of a Dominican monastery and the baroque altars sparkled with gold and gilt. It was almost unbelievably ornate. However, what really fascinated me was the ceiling just inside the entrance.

The ceiling background was white and superimposed on this was the family tree of Santo Domingo de Guzman, the 13th century monk who founded the Dominican order. The branches of the tree bore green leaves, coloured fruit and golden flowers but from each flower rose the colourfully clothed upper torso, head and arms of a family member. From the way these figures were dressed and what they were holding, we were able to deduce that Santo Domingo's relatives and ancestors had included royalty, warriors, monks, merchants and farmers. A bench had been provided and I sat for a long time gazing upwards, absolutely enchanted by this wonderful ceiling.

Outside the church was a large courtyard, shaded by beautiful trees with fronded leaves bearing scarlet flowers and long hanging seed pods. We sat here for a while to rest and write a few postcards and then continued further up the street. Here we found a broad flight of steps between the houses, almost completely covered by market stalls selling materials and clothing. Blue cotton awnings provided some shade from the afternoon heat but there were few customers. Several women stallholders were sitting on the pavement and making use of their time by weaving brightly coloured lengths of cloth using small handlooms.

There was a narrow gap between the stalls and we walked up the steps to find ourselves in another small square, full of market stalls. These were mostly selling textiles but we also saw some of the brightly painted twisty wood carvings that seemed peculiar to this area and stalls selling straw hats, bags and pottery. Much of the pottery was black, a speciality of this region, and included pots of varying shapes and sizes with designs cut out of the sides. I assumed that these were intended to hold candles and let the light shine through but their purpose may have been purely ornamental.

On one side of the square was a building bearing the name 'Artisana Cocijo' which was closed but which we thought may be a showroom. It was painted a bright aquamarine, with an emerald green awning over the entrance and an arrangement of clay pots outside. Nearby, against the wall, hung a large selection of woven rugs with white tasselled ends. Most of these had patterns made up of a combination of stripes and diamonds but a few had more individual designs of animals, birds or fish.

As we made our way slowly back in the direction of the zocalo, exploring arcades, entrances and side streets on the way, we came across a Cartography Museum. Like most of the buildings in Oaxaca, this was built around a courtyard, hidden from view from the pavement. The various rooms around the courtyard contained local maps dating back to the 16th century. "This looks interesting," I said. "Yes," David agreed. "Let's go in."

The museum turned out to be a fascinating place. We were the only visitors so the curator had time to talk to us. He explained, "When the Spaniards arrived in the 16th century, they claimed all the land other than what the local Indians could prove was their property, as shown on a site plan. The Indians were uneducated and did not know how to draw maps. In their sketches, they first put in all the local landmarks such as hills, rivers and mountains and then drew the houses, churches and other buildings, much as a child would draw them." This had resulted in a collection of very picturesque maps of the 16th century villages of the area, some more sophisticated than others.

The curator and museum provided a wealth of information. We learned that during the late 19th century, Mexico was ruled with an iron fist by Porfirio Diaz, who kept the country free from civil war and brought it into the industrial age but at the expense of a loss of freedom. There was a ban on political opposition, free elections and a free press, peasants were cheated out of their land and many resources passed into foreign ownership. In 1911, the Zapatista movement called for the restoration of land to the peasants. This land reform and distribution took place gradually over the next twenty years. Ownership again had to be proved and some peasants used the original 16th century maps that had been passed down through their families for generations, while others drew their own maps. Most of the maps in the museum came into the possession of the Government during this period.

After we left the museum, we passed blocks of student flats belonging to Oaxaca University and we found numerous shopping arcades and several restaurants, each with its own central courtyard.

We were impressed by one which had tables in the courtyard, flowers hanging from the first floor balcony and an array of statues around a higher balcony, just below a perspex roof. We went inside and David asked a couple at one of the tables, "What's the food like here?" "It's very good," they said. "We come here quite often. Why not try it?"

"Are you ready for a meal yet?" David asked me. "I wouldn't mind eating here." It was only about 6 pm but that evening, at 7.30 pm, we were going to a show with the group and Peter had suggested that we eat beforehand. "It's a good idea," I concurred. "It will give us time to shower and change back at the hotel before we go out tonight." We sat and ordered and found that the service was good and the food delicious.

That evening, we all met in the lobby and Peter took us to the nearby Monte Alban Hotel to see a display of folk dancing from different parts of Mexico. There were ten very varied folk dances and the performance was excellent with spectacular costumes, particularly for the finale, an Aztec feather dance.

As we made our way back to our hotel, a political rally was taking place in the zocalo, with a lot of shouting through loudspeakers accompanied by very loud pop music. A few people were dancing but the majority just stood around watching and listening. "What a noise," David yelled to me over the din. "There's no point in going back to our room while this is going on."

We stood with the locals, watching the dancers and being deafened. Luckily the rally finished at 11 pm and the zocalo gradually emptied so we returned to the hotel and retired for the night.

Thursday 3rd July

The next morning, our bags had to be packed and down in the lobby by 6.30 am. Peter had arranged for the hotel to provide us all with a packed breakfast, as we would be leaving by 7 am when the restaurant opened.

Oaxaca

Santo Domingo Church, Oaxaca

Mitla mosaics

Hall of Columns, Mitla

As we set off, Peter told us, "This will be our longest day for travelling as we have to cover a distance of five hundred and sixty six kilometres from Oaxaca to our next destination, Chiapa del Corzo. There will be at least six hours driving but don't worry, we'll break the journey. We have a couple of stops scheduled on the way."

Our first stop was at Santa Maria El Tule, only ten kilometres from Oaxaca. The village of Santa Maria was very pretty with mountains in the background and a large area of parkland in the centre, full of flowers. The driver parked the coach and we got out. "Follow me," said Peter.

The streets were full of large beetles, mostly lying on their backs, waving their legs in the air. "Ugh," shuddered Kayleigh, trying to pick her way through them. "They look like enormous cockroaches." "Ignore them, they're only scarab beetles," said Cheryl dismissively. "Don't worry, Kayleigh," Lynn said more sympathetically. "We see a lot of these in Australia. They're supposed to be lucky."

As we reached a corner of the street, an apparently demented Alsatian dog was barking loudly and rushing around the roof of a single-storey building that turned out to be the General Store and Post Office. "A lot of guard dogs in Mexico live on the roof of the property they're protecting," Peter told us. "Look, see that enormous tree across the road? That's El Tule. That's what we've come here to look at."

"El Tule is an ahuehuete tree, a type of cypress," Peter said, once we had walked over to it and were standing under its spreading branches. "It's said to be at least two thousand years old but could well be older and a feast is held in its honour in October every year. Cortes is supposed to have stopped and dined under this tree when he was marching from Mexico City to conquer Central America. Its trunk is forty two metres in circumference and it apparently has the largest girth of any tree in the Americas."

I had to walk across the square to fit the tree into the viewfinder of my camera. It stood near a church and from that perspective, the bell towers appeared to reach only about a third of the way up the tree canopy. Neville stood in front of the railings surrounding the tree while Diane took a photograph with the tree trunk in the background and he looked really small and insignificant in contrast. Despite its age, the tree seemed extremely robust and healthy and was full of birds nesting in its branches and in holes in the trunk. The birdsong was nearly deafening.

When we had all viewed the tree from every angle, we made our way back to the coach and continued on our way. We had only been travelling for about an hour when we pulled into a lay-by to look at some more cacti. The pole-like grey-green single stemmed cacti had spread all over the stony hillside between other bushier plants. Right next to the lay-by were two fine examples of prickly pear cacti, the pears a dull red in colour growing all round the top edges of the flat, oval-shaped, thorny leaves.

Kayleigh grabbed the chance to have a quick cigarette. As the only smoker in the group, she found it quite difficult at times to find the opportunity to satisfy her cravings. "I keep telling her to give it up but she won't," Diane said to me. "Sometimes I wonder if it's just to defy me." Peter was now urging us to get back on board. "As soon as you're ready," he said to Kayleigh , "we need to be on our way. We'll be stopping again a short distance down the road." Kayleigh regretfully stubbed out her cigarette and followed the rest of us on to the coach.

We had only travelled about a further kilometre when we reached the town of Mitla. "We are about to see the remains of another Zapotec city," Peter told us. "You'll find it completely different from Monte Alban." We stopped in a large cobbled square beside the Municipal Craft Market. This was housed in a series of long, single storey, rather unattractive concrete buildings with a few satellite dishes on the roofs. There was no time to see what they were selling as Peter hurried us through to the site of the ruins.

Here, the single stemmed pole-like cacti had been put to good use, as a single row of them had been grown closely together around the boundary of the site, with other cacti poles tied across them to form a sturdy living fence and barrier. The entry was beside a red-domed church and here we met our new guide, Rosa, a dark haired attractive woman in her early forties, who took us round the site.

"Mitla was a Zapotec settlement from as early as 100 AD," she said. "I understand you have already visited Monte Alban." We nodded. "After the decline of Monte Alban in about 750 AD, Mitla became increasingly important and was one of the main Zapotec centres. It was here that the high priest arranged religious ceremonies and human sacrifices. He used the movements of the stars and planets to advise on the most propitious times, for example, to plant crops or gather in the harvest. Although Mitla was briefly taken over by the Mixtecs in the 14th century and was also conquered by the Aztecs in 1494, it was still occupied by Zapotecs when the Spaniards arrived in the 16th century."

As she led us through the site, we noticed that the walls were decorated with friezes of clear, sharp geometric designs standing proud of the background stonework and, while some looked a little worn, the majority looked as though they had been renovated recently. Some of the patterns were interlocking and looked quite complicated, many with saw-tooth edges.

"These designs are all Zapotec in origin," explained Rosa. "As you go round the site, you will find that there are fourteen different designs. Rather than being carved from the main stone, each pattern is made up of tiny pieces of rock, cut and shaped to fit the design before being attached to the wall. The smooth stonework below and between the geometric patterns was first covered in stucco and painted and the designs would then have been painted in contrasting colours."

When we looked closely at the designs, we could see the little individual stones, like mosaic bricks, those making the saw-tooth designs all identical in length, width, depth and angle of cut. Diamonds were shaped from what looked like tiny rectangular identical toy bricks. It would have required endless patience to shape each of those tiny pieces of stone by hand and then to fit them into the patterns on the walls.

"We think each group of buildings was reserved for specific occupants, one for the King, one for the High Priest, one for lesser priests, one for officials, and so on," Rosa told us. She pointed to what was left of a red pattern painted on a pink background above one of the doors. "We believe the hieroglyphs above the doors gave the history of those who occupied the premises."

Along the north side of the Northern Patio, a building more than a hundred feet long stood on a platform and was reached by a broad flight of steps between red-painted walls. This building had three large entrances. On either side of these were three pairs of horizontal decorative panels, each containing a different geometric design and separated from the other panels by plain smooth stonework, the centre pair of panels protruding and slightly higher than the pairs on either side of them. There were further decorative panels between and above the doors. Along the edge of the roof, more decorative panels were placed at intervals. It must have been very impressive when the whole façade was painted, with the designs standing out in contrast to the background colour.

Inside the building was the Hall of the Columns. This was a long rectangular room down the length of which, to the right of centre, stood a row of six smooth squat pillars. Rosa led us down a passage from here into the Patio of the Mosaics. "This Patio is considered to contain some of Mitla's best stonework," she said proudly. We were given as much time as we wanted to look around. In places, different geometric designs lay one above the other, separated only by a single narrow stone tile. Some parts of the dog-tooth design had been coloured a deep yellow ochre.

Rosa then took us into a small room off the Patio. "This room has had a wooden roof fitted, constructed to the original design," she told us. "At one time, all the buildings had wooden roofs like this." There were no windows and it was too dark to see how the roof was put together but rooms such as this no doubt provided welcome shelter from the heat and rain.

We then went over to the Southern Patio where there were two underground tombs. "At one time, the High Priests and officials from Monte Alban were brought all the way to Mitla to be buried and for this reason, Mitla is known as 'The Place of the Dead'," Rosa told us. "Somewhere beneath the modern city, there is said to be an enormous burial site containing the remains of Zapotec kings and their greatest priests and warriors but this has not yet been found."

The entrances to the tombs were very restricted and quite difficult to negotiate. Steps led down to a low narrow tunnel with burial chambers off to either side like a catacomb and steps up again at the other end. In one of the tombs was a large stone column. "This is the Column of Life," said Rosa. "If you put your arms around it, the number of hand widths between your finger tips is supposed to measure how many years you still have left to live." "I'll try that," said Ian. Because he was tall and thin with very long arms, he could almost touch his fingers together round the back of the pillar and, according to the legend, clearly had a very short life expectancy. Perhaps this belief was more relevant to the Zapotecs, who would probably have been delighted at the thought that they may be chosen for sacrifice in only a year or two.

"Talking about not having long to live," said Peter, "I was out here at the start of November last year when Mexico celebrated the Day of the Dead. I found it quite amazing. The church bells are rung throughout the previous night to waken the dead and the next day, everyone goes to the churchyard with food and drink for their dead relatives and has a party. Bands play in the cemeteries, people dance and have picnics round the graves and the shops and market stalls all sell skull masks and coffins and skulls made of chocolate and sugar candy. It's quite macabre."

As we left the site, we looked inside the attractive stone church with the red domes that stood by the entrance. This was the Church of San Pablo and it appeared to have been decorated for a religious festival or possibly a wedding. The lower part of the golden altar was almost hidden by tall vases filled with red, white and yellow flowers, mainly roses, daisies and chrysanthemums, while spaced along the full width of the steps leading to the altar were more tall vases containing pink and white gladioli. Between the vases was the glow of lighted candles.

Above the altar steps, an arch led to a dome above the altar and red and white streamers hung from the centre of this arch. All the statues around the church were richly dressed. One statue of the Madonna, standing on a triangular gold pedestal on the wall, wore a black satin dress patterned with silver sequins in an abstract design of angels and stars. Over this was a long black satin cloak edged in gold braid and the hair was covered by a lace cap under a golden crown. It looked beautiful.

From here we returned to the coach and set off again. We had detoured from the main road to visit Mitla and we now drove back to this road. As we continued eastwards, our journey took us through wooded hills and mountains where buzzards hung in the sky searching for prey and huge yellow, white and orange butterflies flitted across the road.

We came down to a flat sandy plain where, at 2.30 pm, we stopped to eat at a restaurant adjoining a petrol station. The heat here was oppressive and all David and I wanted for lunch were cold drinks and a few biscuits left over from our picnic two days earlier. "We will soon reach the spot where the Pacific Ocean curves upwards towards the Gulf of Mexico to create an isthmus. There is usually a breeze there that makes it feel cooler," Peter encouraged us.

When the road eventually took us through the narrowest stretch of land from north to south, several motionless windmills confirmed that the air was just as still. The other road traffic was mainly commercial but we saw some public transport trucks with all the passengers standing in the back and some Army vehicles with guns mounted at front and rear, manned by soldiers ready to open fire.

As we neared the border with the State of Chiapas, we left the plain and drove between green hills with wooded lower slopes and bare grassy tops that, to me, looked almost exactly like the hills and mountains of the English Lake District. The scenery may have improved but the road had deteriorated badly. As we climbed higher into the mountains, our driver tried to keep to the centre of the highway because there were places where the edge of the road had simply slipped away down the hillside into the valley below.

Kayleigh was in the seat just behind the driver where she had a clear view in front. She was getting really agitated about the state of the road, perhaps picturing it giving way as we were driving over it. "Oh no," she cried out as we approached a particularly bad stretch. "Look at that! The road's gone altogether!"

As the driver detoured on to a temporary track cut into the side of the hill, we could see that a whole section of road, about twenty feet long, had broken away completely. "I can't take this," said Kayleigh and she moved to a seat towards the rear of the coach.

As we crossed the border into Chiapas State, the road improved instantly and Kayleigh went back into her seat at the front where she had a better view. We had only travelled a few miles when we were flagged down by two policemen who demanded to see the driver's documentation. They checked this carefully and then insisted on having details of the tour group, where we had come from and our destination. After a discussion lasting about ten minutes, the driver was fined ten pesos, the equivalent of about one British pound, and we were allowed to continue on our journey.

Once we were safely moving again, we asked Peter what the problem was. "As far as I know, there was no problem," he said, having been listening in to the conversation between the policemen and the driver. "The police are paid very low salaries and they provide themselves with extra income by imposing small fines in this way."

The weather had now deteriorated from the blazing hot sunshine of midday and it was raining hard. Our driver slowed right down and Peter pointed out a sign warning of falling rocks. "This is the most hazardous part of the journey," he cautioned. In the past, we had often seen signs reading 'Danger. Beware of Falling Rocks' with a diagram of rocks tumbling down a cliff face but, although we were aware of the possibility of this happening, we had never actually expected any rocks to drop on us. Here it was different.

This stretch of road had been cut between high sandy cliffs and the heavy rain was washing away the sand. Through the window, I could see rocks teetering on the very edge of the cliff and as I watched, a boulder hurtled downhill and crashed on to the road in front of us. As the driver braked and then swerved round it, Kayleigh screamed and then covered her face with her hands. "I can't look," she whispered. Neville and Diane sat across the gangway from us and we could see them bracing themselves against the back of the seat in front and looking very worried. Rocks of varying sizes already littered the road and a lump of rock bounced off the roof of the car in front of us, leaving a dent. Our driver braked sharply as another large boulder rolled down the cliff. David and I felt more excited than worried, as events were out of our control and we had to trust our driver to bring us through safely. He was peering upwards, alternately braking and accelerating and weaving in and out around the boulders, some of which were nearly as large as a small car. The journey may have been long but it was certainly not boring.

Luckily the cutting was only about half a mile long and we were soon out of the danger zone but the driver must have been relieved when the coach finally reached its destination, the town of Chiapa del Corzo, with no more than a few scratches.

3

CHIAPA DEL CORZO AND THE SUMIDERO CANYON

We stopped outside a small three storey hotel called La Ceiba. Peter checked us all in at Reception, handed out the room keys and said, "You have fifteen minutes to shower and change and then I'll meet you here in the lobby at a quarter to eight. We can walk to a restaurant in the town centre for our evening meal." The rain had now stopped but David and I were feeling tired after the journey and wanted to take it easy, so we told Peter we would eat at the hotel which had its own restaurant on the second floor.

Consequently, we took our time getting ready and went into the restaurant at eight o'clock that evening. There was one other couple in there, in their thirties. We sat at the table next to theirs and discovered that they were English and part of another tour group. They had travelled that afternoon along the same route as we had and their coach had actually been hit by a rock, large enough to dent the roof and damage some of the cases tied on top. They were feeling a little shaken so had decided not to go out that evening.

The restaurant was very bare and lacked character but the food was good and we were entertained by a green gecko running round the wall making clicking noises. We were about halfway through the meal when the heavens opened and we listened to the rain hammering on the roof and windows. "I'm so glad we decided to stay and eat here," said David. As lightning flashed and thunder rumbled loudly around us, the rest of us had to agree.

After the meal, the four of us went to the small bar area downstairs and sat chatting and drinking coffee. At about ten o'clock, the rest of our group arrived back at the hotel, absolutely drenched. Most of them were barefoot and carrying their shoes and socks.

"We went to a restaurant in the zocalo and we were eating our meal when the storm started," Garry told us. "The zocalo is in the lowest part of the town and the water gushes down into the square from all the side streets. The restaurant stayed dry but as we came out, we found that the water in the square was more than a foot deep. We had to wade through it to get back to the hotel." "We all took off our shoes and socks and tried to roll up our trousers but they still got wet," moaned Sue. "I need a hot shower." "Me too," said Lynn. "I'm only hoping our clothes dry out by the morning."

As our friends went upstairs grumbling, David and I thanked our lucky stars once again that we had decided against going with them that evening.

Friday 4th July

Although we were only at Chiapa del Corzo for one night, we were not leaving until eleven o'clock the following morning. David and I had an early breakfast in the restaurant and then set off to explore the town. As we walked downhill towards the zocalo, we saw that the kerbs on either side of the road were more than a foot high and we now knew the reason for this. We tried to walk on the pavement but this was in short lengths, divided at every house entrance by a slope from the door to the road. After climbing up and down the high kerb a few times, we gave up and walked in the road instead. The houses were single storey buildings painted in pastel shades of pink, green and blue, mostly with a door and single window facing on to the street.

When we reached the zocalo, we saw a garden in the centre of the square. Its main feature was a 16th century fountain covered by what was supposedly a brick replica of the Spanish crown. This had a central pink segmented dome and cupola supported by an octagon of arches with eight half-arches spread out around it, each with a little turret on its outer support wall. Wide paved paths were separated by patches of greenery, where the foliage of several trees and shrubs had been clipped into circular horizontal disks on trunks. Each of these living wheels was full of very noisy birds.

We walked round the zocalo past a school with mesh over the windows instead of glass and the children all called out to us as we went by. On the far side of the zocalo was a covered arcade and next to this, a large covered market. We looked in the windows of the arcade shops and stopped outside one displaying the most beautiful hand-embroidered blouses, dresses and waistcoats. "I like those," said David, gazing at the waistcoats. "I wonder if they have anything in my size." "When would you wear it?" I asked. "At Helen's wedding next month, for a start." Helen was the daughter of our closest friends and we had been invited to the wedding in Newcastle, followed by the reception to be held in a Northumbrian castle.

We went into the shop and the assistant told us that the embroidered clothing was a speciality of this area. David asked about the waistcoats and she brought some out for him to try on. They were gorgeous but they were all too short in the back. The assistant then told him tactfully that, although men did wear the waistcoats, they were really intended for women. It was quite a disappointment.

As we went into the market, it was already hot so David bought himself a hat with a large brim for ten pesos, to keep the sun off his face and neck. Everyone in the market was very friendly and invited us to try all kinds of herbs and spices. The women on the stalls were charmed by David and one of them stuffed some herbs in his shirt pocket. He accepted them as he did not want to hurt her feelings but took them out of his pocket as soon as he could and amazed a woman shopper at the far end of the market by presenting them to her with a flourish.

Peter had suggested that we look for gifts for children at two schools we would be visiting in Guatemala, later in the holiday. After toying with the idea of buying various items, from notepaper and biros to sweets, we decided that pencils were more practical as they would probably last longer than pens, so we bought a few packs of these. We also bought some balloons and some packets of mixed dried fruit and nuts, which we thought would be healthier than sweets.

As we left the market, we could see across the road the 16th century bell tower of the Temple of Santo Domingo. We looked inside the church but to us, it looked nothing out of the ordinary, although we were told that the bell in the tower dated back to 1576 and was made of gold, silver and copper.

Beside the church was a small library and next to it what we thought would be an equally small museum. "We can't go inside anyway," I said. "It doesn't open until eleven o'clock and we have to be back at the hotel before then." An elderly man was tidying the grass area in front and overheard me. "You can go inside now if you would like to," he said. "I have the keys here." "Oh, that would be wonderful," I said, taken by surprise and accepting the keys. "Thank you very much."

Inside the entrance, a flight of stairs led to the first floor museum but first we went through an archway which took us into the old church cloisters. Here we walked through a lovely garden of pillars and archways. The arches near the entrance were in red brick but the inner arches were covered in smooth red plaster with a narrow border of white stonework round the top of each of the pillars. On the inside curve of some of the upper arches, the plaster had been cut away to reveal a design of large white stucco flowers on a light brown background, the red centres of the flowers matching the plaster. These red arches surrounded a square of lush grass and mature trees in the middle of which was an ancient stone fountain. Small potted palms had been placed in the centre of some of the archways. Flights of house martins were wheeling overhead catching insects and it was delightful to stand there for a few moments, watching them from the dappled shade of the trees.

From here, we went upstairs to the museum, the door to which was already open. Inside we found a collection of lacquered gourds, another speciality of this area, and wooden furniture decorated with detailed lacquered flower designs. A craftswoman sat on a chair painting a gourd bowl and, although we were there early, she did not appear surprised to see us. We would have liked to have stayed for a while to watch her at work but it was now time for us to return the keys and make our way back to the hotel.

As we passed the entrance to the covered market, we saw that some very colourful flower stalls had been erected across the pavement and at the side of the road. When we reached the school at the far end of the zocalo, some of the children were out in the playground, practising a formal dance to some rather tinny music from a loudspeaker. We stopped for a moment at the entrance and the teacher beckoned to us. "Come inside and watch," she called. "Thank you, we would love to but, unfortunately, we don't have time," we shouted back and continued quickly on our way.

Back at the hotel, we hurried to our bedroom overlooking a small swimming pool, where several of our friends later told us they had spent the morning, and we brought our cases down, ready to be loaded on to the bus waiting outside. This was much smaller than the coach we had been using previously and all the cases had to be piled on the back seats.

This left just enough room for us all to sit down, although Garry and I were both perched over the wheels with our knees up under our chins. "Sorry about the cramped conditions, folks," said Peter cheerily as we drove away, "but you'll be getting off again in a few minutes. We're just going down to the river."

From the coach park where we left the bus, the road dipped steeply down to the jetty and there were souvenir stalls on either side. "Have a look round here while I go and buy our tickets for the river trip to the Sumidero Canyon," Peter told us. We wandered slowly down the hill. The stallholders were clearly anticipating a lucrative tourist trade because everything was very expensive and we found that postcards here were twice the price of those in town.

A young man came over to us and tried to chat up Sue, with some help from Diane who spoke a little Spanish. "He says you are very beautiful and is asking if you are a model," translated Diane. "He thinks you look just like Princess Diana." Sue may have been flattered but she remained looking cool, distant and uninterested. The young man then said to Diane, "I don't suppose a girl like her would consider talking to a man like me." Diane translated this into English for Sue who retorted sarcastically, "It would be a little difficult since we don't speak the same language." The whole group was listening in to this fascinating exchange when our speedboat arrived at the jetty. Peter called us and Sue left her would-be suitor without a backward glance.

Once we were settled on board, Peter asked, "Is there anyone here who can't swim?" Much to his surprise, two of the group raised their hands. "Well, accidents have been known on this stretch of river," he warned us. "I must insist that you all wear your lifejackets." As we put them on, we could see the passengers in the boat next to ours grinning and pointing but we thought, "Better be safe than sorry."

We set off upstream, under a bridge and round a bend to the start of the canyon, taking it at a gentle pace. The speedboat which had been next to ours on the jetty zipped past with the passengers still laughing at us for our timidity. We were glad of the slower speed as it gave us time to look at the scenery. It was hot and sticky and we appreciated the cooling breeze from our movement across the water.

"You are now on the Rio Grijalva, named after one of the 16th century Spanish invaders, and you are about to enter the Sumidero Canyon," Peter told us. "This canyon is about forty kilometres long and the water is said to be up to three hundred metres deep in places. At the far end there's a lake, formed after a dam was constructed nearly twenty years ago, but we are only going as far as the highest, most dramatic part of the canyon." As the river narrowed between the cliffs, the rock walls seemed to close in on us from either side. The sky was overcast, it was slightly hazy and the atmosphere felt sombre and oppressive.

The river twisted and turned between the canyon walls and then we approached a very narrow stretch where the cliffs rose almost sheer from the water. "The sides of the canyon here are more than a thousand metres high," Peter told us. After a quick calculation, David said in awe, "That's higher than Scafell Pike." "I know that's the highest mountain in England but how high is it?" I asked, knowing that David keeps these odd snippets of information in his head. "Three thousand two hundred and ten feet," he replied. "I make that about nine hundred and ninety metres."

"The Chiapa Indians once had their capital near here on the far side of the river," Peter continued. "See that cliff in front of you? In 1528, hundreds of Chiapa Indians, men, women and children, hurled themselves into the canyon from the highest point, preferring to face certain death in the river rather than suffer shame and defeat under the conquering Spaniards." We could just imagine it and the atmosphere became, if possible, even more sombre.

Just beyond this cliff, our speedboat turned and we headed back towards Chiapa del Corzo. Travelling in this direction, we could see an opening like a small cave high up on the cliff face on our right. A ladder led to the cave entrance from halfway up the cliff and just inside the cave was a small white plinth on which stood a statuette of the Virgin Mary, surrounded by what looked like white vases holding artificial red roses. "How do people get up there?" asked Sam. "Before the dam was built, the water level of the Rio Grijalva would rise by more than a hundred feet in the rainy season," Peter told us. "At those times, people would have easy access to the shrine from the river. It would be very difficult to reach it now."

Great islands of water hyacinths floated on the river and as we passed these, we slowed right down to look at nesting herons and egrets. Trees grew wherever they could get a foothold on the sides of the cliffs and cormorants perched on dead branches growing out over the water, their wings spread wide, occasionally swooping down to take a fish. We saw pelicans flying swiftly across the river in small groups of twos or threes and then we spotted some balancing on the higher tree branches. "Look at those," I said to David. "I somehow never thought of pelicans sitting in trees."

"Look up there," called Ian. "Isn't that a vulture?" "Where? I can't see it." "Just up there where those two bare branches are sticking out." We followed the direction in which he was pointing and saw the vulture sitting there, recognisable from its hunched shoulders and bare 'U-bend' neck. "Look, there's another one," cried Alan.

While we were looking for more birds, our skipper brought the boat in towards a waterfall running down the cliff face. "This is known as the Christmas Tree," said Peter and we saw that moss and tufa had grown out from the rock face in large curved fronds, hollow underneath. Seen from the right angle, it was possible to imagine the outline of a Christmas tree. This was clearly one of the major sights of the canyon as we paused for a few moments for photographs, our captain steering the speedboat as close as possible to the cliff so we could feel the spray from the waterfall.

As we set off again, a large vessel was travelling slowly in the opposite direction, piled high with water hyacinths. "It's a never-ending job to clear this weed from the river," said Peter, "but if it was left, it would soon block the waterway completely. There's an area near the dam where the water hyacinth plants are collected and turned into compost."

A little further downstream Peter said, "Keep your eyes peeled here for crocodiles. They are often found along this stretch of the river." Our skipper slowed the boat again and as other craft sped past us, we all studied the banks closely and were rewarded eventually with the sighting of two crocodiles, an adult basking on a narrow grassy bank that ignored us and a young one, judging from its size, that crawled hurriedly into the river as we passed.

By the time we arrived back at the jetty, it was lunchtime and Peter took us to a little restaurant where we could sit outside on the river bank. Although we were the only customers, the waiter had to look around for extra chairs to seat all thirteen of us. As he handed out some flimsy hand-written menus, he said, "I recommend the fresh river fish." "I'd rather have pizza," said Ian. "Me too," agreed Kayleigh.

The rest of us went with the recommendation and ordered fish. Later, we found out that the kitchen consisted of one woman using a single frying pan over an open fire. She had a clay oven for the pizzas but could only cook two fish at a time in her pan and it took about an hour before we were all served. We had tapas and salad with the fish which was tasty but not very filling. We then returned to our small cramped bus for the journey to San Cristobal de las Casas, which fortunately only took a couple of hours, with rain and rockets accompanying us for most of the way.

Spanish fountain, Chiapa del Corzo

Sumidero Canyon

Christmas tree formation

Church, San Juan Chamula

Tzotzil Indian girl

Clothing on sale at Zinacantan

4

SAN CRISTOBAL DE LAS CASAS

As we drove into the city, Peter handed out maps and informed us that in the 19th century, San Cristobal de las Casas had been the State capital of Chiapas. "You'll find it's a beautiful colonial town with plenty of atmosphere," he said. "It stands at a height of about 2,200 metres in the Chiapas Mountains and Indians come into the town from the surrounding villages to buy and sell goods in the market. These include the Tzotzil and Tzeltal Indians who still have their own language."

He continued, "Many people consider that these Indians have had a raw deal from the Government. In 1994, San Cristobal was captured by the Zapatista National Liberation Army who were standing up for the rights of Mexico's oppressed Indians. The Mexican army quickly quelled the rebellion but the fact that they had lost the city at all shocked the Mexican government into promising to look into the Indians' grievances."

Our hotel was not far from the city centre and was built around two courtyards. One of these was paved, with a central fountain surrounded by red-brown clay pots. The other had a stone path round a lawn, with an earth mound in the centre on which pots were decoratively arranged. A tall white pot with a frilly edge stood at the top of the mound surrounded by pots in different shapes and sizes in white, brick-red and dark grey, interspersed with ornamental shrubs and ground cover plants.

From the two courtyards, steps led to the first floor walkways which were enhanced by wrought iron designs and smiling pottery suns. It was a most attractive place but the rain had stopped as we arrived, the rest of the afternoon was free and we had a new town to explore. As soon as our cases had been unloaded from the bus and we had taken them up to our room, David and I set off to find the zocalo.

This was only a short distance away and held some shady trees and the cathedral, its outside brightly painted in salmon pink and yellow. From here, we walked uphill towards the old town. This was clearly a tourist centre with many lovely shops, including several which sold cameras and film.

David was still fascinated by the embroidered waistcoats and we went into one or two shops to see what was available. He was very tempted to buy one in a rich crushed black satin, embroidered with dark crimson flowers, but regretfully decided against it because it was still a little too short for him. In another shop, I tried on a lovely pair of Hush Puppy leather walking shoes with deep-ridged soles, being offered at a bargain price, but they were unfortunately a little too narrow for my large broad feet. Wrought iron signs and crosses seemed to be a speciality in this area. As we climbed higher up the hill, we had excellent views across to the green, hillocky mountains surrounding the town.

The road was steep and we were soon feeling tired but that evening, having had a short rest at the hotel, we decided to walk back up the hill to a restaurant we had seen earlier. Here we had pork chops, David's with a jacket potato, mine with frijoles, a very tasty and filling bean dish. It was an excellent meal.

Saturday 5th July

The next morning, after a leisurely breakfast, we set off as a group at 9 am with Peter leading the way uphill through the old town. We crossed a very busy market area where local farmers had spread their wares across the narrow pavements and out into the roadway on either side. The streets were a seething mass of pedestrians mingling with traffic which moved at a snail's pace, trying to force its way through. The group found it impossible to stay together so those at the front watched which way Peter was taking us and waved and signalled to those behind.

Eventually, some distance from the market, we came to a combi parking area. A combi was a cross between a large taxi and a minibus and held eight passengers. Peter arranged for two of these to take us to San Juan Chamula, an Indian village in the mountains. As we set off on the road out of town, we found our combi quite comfortable and roomy.

A few miles into the countryside, we suddenly came to a halt. Our driver got out and waved down the other combi which stopped behind us. "What's happened?" asked Ian. "I don't know," said David. "Let's get out and see." As everybody climbed out of both combis, we found that our vehicle had suffered a burst tyre. There was very little other traffic but as two more vehicles approached, one from either direction, these were waved down as well and the drivers came over to find out what the problem was and to assist.

It took four drivers to change the wheel while we stood at the side of the road, watching proceedings. One man piled rocks behind the back wheels while two jacked up the vehicle and the fourth loosened the wheel nuts. With teamwork, the job was soon finished and we were once again on our way to San Juan Chamula.

The combis were parked on the outskirts of the village and as we got out, Peter warned us, "The people here are Tzotzil Indians. Please be very careful not to photograph anybody without getting their permission first, as many believe that having their likeness taken will steal their souls."

As we walked towards the village centre, most of the adults hid their faces or went into their houses and they were all firmly against having their photographs taken. However, the children were all only too happy to sell their souls for a small amount of money and they surrounded us, begging us to take photographs of them. Older children were responsible for looking after their younger siblings and nearly every young girl had a small child hanging in a blanket on her back.

Peter led us to the centre of the village and stopped in front of the church, which was painted a pristine white with turquoise green decorations. Three bells hung in openings at the top of the façade. A rope was attached to the building just below the centre bell, while another rope was fastened to one side of a tall, narrow arched balcony above the main door. Both ropes were draped across the church frontage, their ends being anchored on either side of the building. It was not clear whether the ropes were for ringing the bells or whether they were decorative.

"You will be going into the church in a moment," said Peter. "You can take as many pictures of the building as you like out here but please remember that photographs are forbidden inside. I think you'll find it interesting. Although Chamula is in a Catholic area, it has its own version of Mayan Catholicism and has been excommunicated by the Pope. As in other parts of Mexico, the villagers believe that Christ rose from the Cross to become the Sun, the Virgin Mary is the Moon and the saints are accepted as the equivalent of the old Mayan gods. Here, however, a new priest is elected on 1st January each year and Carnival celebrations before the start of Lent mark the balancing days of the old Mayan calendar."

As we stood there, some villagers walked past carrying hens which they took inside the church. Peter continued, "You'll find people making various offerings to the saints. These include chickens and Coca Cola." "Coca cola?" queried Kayleigh with a giggle. "Coca Cola is revered here," Peter told her, "because the Indians believe that, when the gases from the drink cause burping, this is actually driving evil spirits from the body. There are two large Coca Cola warehouses in this one small village alone." "I'll never think the same way about burping again," laughed Garry.

As we walked up to the entrance door, Peter said, "I won't come in with you because I've seen inside before. You'll have to pay as you go into the church and you may be asked to make further payments once you are inside, depending which parts of the church you want to visit. You can take as long as you want and you should have enough time to wander round the village as well. Please meet back at the combi at 11 am."

We paid at the door and entered the church. This was a fascinating building. Hanging from the ceiling down the centre of the church, equally spaced between the door and the altar at the far end, were four broad lengths of white material. These were draped across to the walls on either side and a row of white paper lanterns was suspended from where they were attached to the ceiling. Palm leaves decorated the walls and the floor was strewn with pine needles that gave off a sweet aroma as people walked over them.

The altar at the front was completely covered with flowers, candles and the statues of ten saints, while the statues of many more saints stood in glass cases along the walls on either side, down the full length of the building. There were no pews in this church. Instead, people knelt on the floor and set up their own rows of lighted candles, parallel to the front altar, before making offerings which included eggs, Coca Cola, vegetables and the live chickens we had seen earlier. When I asked Peter about this afterwards, he confirmed that after making their offerings, the Indians would take them back home again for their own use.

We found that if we did not want to remain at the back of the church, we were allowed forward in a roped off section to one side, advancing in stages upon production of further payments. This we did not mind as it helped to bring money to the Indians and we thought that the church, with its scent of pine needles and its flowers, candles, statues and unusual offerings, was a magical place. When we eventually left, we had a short time to wander round the market before returning to our vehicle.

From San Juan Chamula, we went to another village, Zinacantan, less visited by tourists. As we arrived, Peter warned us that here, they were far more strict about photographs. "If you want to take a picture," he said, "you must make your intentions very clear beforehand and wait until anyone in view has hidden behind a wall or inside a building."

This was a great pity because everybody here was dressed in the most beautiful colourful clothes. Most of the women wore heavily embroidered shawls over embroidered blouses while the men wore black ponchos covered with brightly coloured embroidered flowers. The men also wore palm leaf hats that peaked in the centre, had colourful patterns woven into the brim and were threaded at the back of the peak with a rainbow mix of ribbons which hung down from under the back of the brim. "The women can tell which of the men are married from their hats," said Peter. "The single men have broader, longer ribbons."

Peter took us to the village centre and the church. "The people of Zinacantan venerate geraniums and they offer these with pine branches in special rituals to bring all kinds of benefits," he told us. The church here was a long white building, much larger than that in Chamula, with a chapel alongside, a courtyard and a white surrounding wall with an impressive arched entrance.

The church was guarded by a group of young men, all wearing red silk tabards over white shirts. These tabards were almost completely covered in embroidered and appliquéd flowers, with fine fringing along the bottom and three heavy red tassels hanging down each side. Once we had paid them a donation to enter the church, the young men were happy to let us look around by ourselves. Inside this church, in addition to the flowers, candles and statues of saints, there were clay figures of real and mythological animals, both on the altar and all round the edge of the floor.

Although we seemed to be the only visitors to the village, there was a wonderful market of clothes and textiles. The quality of the goods and vibrancy of the colours exceeded any we saw elsewhere during the holiday. These included the beautiful embroidered blouses, shawls and ponchos in which the local people were dressed and some red embroidered tabards, similar to those worn by the young men at the church. There were also beribboned hats, but Peter had warned us against buying and wearing these as it would have been seen as an insult by the locals.

Among the woven goods were tablecloths, curtains and blankets, purses, handbags and bookmarks, all in the most vivid, colourful designs imaginable. "We must buy some of these," said Lynn and she and Alan spent time choosing fabrics for their bottom drawer.

As we returned to San Cristobal de las Casas in the combis, I noticed isolated crosses standing in some of the fields. "Are those crosses marking graves?" I asked Peter. "No," he said. "They indicate the entrances to the dwellings of the ancestor gods and the Earth Lord, the Señor de la Tierra, all of whom have to be kept happy with offerings at appropriate times."

Once back in the town, we were free for the rest of the day. David saw a row of boot boys and as he had been impressed with the way his black shoes had been cleaned in Oaxaca, he decided to take the opportunity to have his brown leather boots cleaned as well. The boot boy did a good job and David gave him a small tip. A gentleman who had been having his shoes cleaned in the next chair came across to us, shook David by the hand, said "I am very honoured to have met you" and walked off, leaving us standing there looking after him in amazement. "I wonder if he was related to the boot boy," I said. "I think he must have mistaken me for somebody else," decided David.

It was now well past lunchtime so we went into a nearby hotel for something to eat and found a lovely red, yellow and black macaw sitting on a perch in the courtyard. There was a very limited menu but we ordered chicken tacos and while we waited for our meal, David started chatting to the couple on the next table. They recommended a visit to an Indian refuge called "Na Bolom", a Tzotzil name meaning "House of the Jaguar". "We went there yesterday," said the woman, rummaging in her bag and bringing out a souvenir leaflet which she quickly scanned. "Look, there's a tour in English this afternoon starting at half past four." She showed us the location on our city map.

We had plenty of time and after the meal, made our way uphill to a church in the old town, the frontage of which was decorated with barley-sugar-twist pillars and statues. In the grounds of the church, a craft market was in full swing so we went to see what was on offer. There were some beautiful leather goods and we were very tempted by some soft suede hides painted with Mayan designs. "They're beautiful but we have nowhere suitable to hang one at home," I said. "I'll try bargaining," decided David. "If we can buy a small one for about £10, we can give it to one of our friends as a present." David is usually good at bargaining but the Indians were holding out for double the price we wanted to pay, so we resisted the temptation.

Following the map, we continued to the top of the hill and down the other side but "Na Bolom" was further away than we thought. Eventually we stopped to ask directions as we began to doubt our own map reading skills. When we finally arrived, we found a house painted in red and yellow ochre and after paying our entrance fees, entered a paved courtyard.

Here, an Indian was sitting on a wooden bench set against the house, holding a small bow and a fan-shaped wooden stand with an array of nine arrows. This Indian wore a short sleeved shapeless white over-garment that reached to just below his knees, looking rather incongruous with a pair of brown brogues and white ankle socks. He had flowing dark curly hair that reached to below his shoulders with a thick curly fringe down to his eyebrows and a thick bushy moustache. He indicated that he was happy for us to take his photograph and we wondered if he was there to sell his bows and arrows, as there were several sets of these propped on the bench beside him. However, he remained silent, so we walked past him into the building, which was a museum.

Here we discovered that "Na Bolom" was founded by Frans Blom, a Danish archaeologist who had worked on the Mayan sites, and his wife, Trudy Duby, a Swiss photographer and anthropologist. Trudy was fascinated by the Indians of Chiapas State, particularly the Lacandon Indians found in the east of Chiapas. She was shocked by the destruction of the Lacandon Rainforest and the exploitation of the Lacandon, Tzotzil and Tzeltal Indian tribes, all direct descendants of the Mayans, and she did whatever she could to preserve their way of life.

Frans Blom died in 1963 while his wife lived until 1993. The museum was full of books, archaeological and anthropological exhibits and photographs taken by Trudy, recording the life of the tribes in the 1950s. A further fifty thousand photographs were stored in a library, opened for studying by appointment only. Many more photographs had been returned to the tribes to enable the children to learn about their tribal history and customs. In the museum, there was also a collection of Indian weapons, clothing, fishing equipment and other items once in everyday use.

Outside in the grounds of the museum were guesthouses made of mud and thatch where any Indian could seek accommodation and refuge, free of charge. The gardens provided enough fruit and vegetables to feed everyone staying there, while a large tree nursery produced young saplings. These were still being used in reforestation projects, although the rainforest was being destroyed far more quickly than it could ever be replaced.

It was the practice of the Mayans to grow crops in one particular area for seven years and then to rest the soil for seven years. Frans and Trudy taught the Indians about crop rotation so that, by using the right combination of crops, they could farm the same land continuously without exhausting the nutrients in the soil, thus reducing the need for further land clearance. We found "Na Bolom" a fascinating and inspiring place to visit.

Afterwards, we went back to the zocalo where, having been unsuccessful in his quest for a richly embroidered waistcoat, David bought one in plain green linen with several pockets. Wearing this with his new wide brimmed hat in the shape of a Stetson, he reminded me of a Texan cowboy and only needed a set of six-shooters.

That day was Garry's birthday and in the evening, to help him to celebrate, Peter took us all to a beautiful restaurant with a balcony. Peter had tried to order a birthday cake, without success, but we had all signed a birthday card, which he presented to Garry with a short speech at the start of the meal. We were enjoying our food and drinks when, just before 9 pm, the restaurant proprietor hurried over looking very agitated.

He spoke rapidly to Peter in Spanish and Peter told us that we must finish any alcohol and remove the evidence within five minutes, as the police were on their way. He then explained, "The elections are being held tomorrow and all voters are required by law to be sober. Most places stopped selling alcohol at six o'clock this evening but the police are keeping a very strict control. If we're found with wine on the table, the restaurant will be heavily fined and could lose its licence."

"If we pour all the red wine into cups, it would look just like black coffee," suggested Sam. "Hey, that's a brilliant idea," said Ian. Peter had a word with the waiter who brought us all cups and saucers and we shared out the rest of the red wine. It was, indeed, indistinguishable in appearance from black coffee, and we thought the police would be unlikely to go to the extreme of smelling it.

In the meantime, we quickly drank the remains of the white wine and beer and the waiter collected up the glasses while we hurriedly hid all the bottles under the table. When the police arrived at 9.15 pm to inspect the restaurant, Peter spoke to them and told them we were tourists so they knew that none of us would be voting in the elections. We did not look drunk and there was no obvious evidence of alcohol being on sale so, after a cursory look around, the police left again. However, this had put rather a damper on the evening and as soon as we had finished our meal, we all decided to return early to the hotel.

Sunday 6th July

The next morning, we had time for a leisurely breakfast before leaving San Cristobal de las Casas at 9.30 am. While the luggage was being loaded into the coach, a group of charming but very persistent young Indian girls were trying to sell their wares, mainly beaded necklaces and bracelets and woven bags, scarves and blankets. In the end, David started getting annoyed with them and they backed off.

As we left San Cristobal, we were at an altitude of nearly 7,000 feet where it was comparatively cool. We had a lovely drive through the mountains and as we dropped down to a lower level, the temperature began to rise. After about two hours, we stopped at a small café with green parrots and a caged baby coati mundi in the garden. The coati mundi with its long twitchy nose was gorgeous, very inquisitive and playful. "I'd like one of those as a pet," I said to David.

San Cristobal de las Casas

Macaw at hotel

Na Bolom

Agua Azul

Path behind Misol-Ha

Also in the garden were the prettiest toilet facilities I had ever seen. The building was sunk into the ground like a bunker, reached by a short flight of steps and almost completely hidden by a very lush pink flowering creeper. These toilets were clean and even had piped running water.

Inside the café, every wall was completely covered with photographs of masked bandits. "Hey, check this out," said Alan, rushing over to look at them. "What's the connection with the café?" asked Sam. After having a word with the café proprietor, Peter told us, "In 1994, the Zapatista Liberation Army captured San Cristobal and neighbouring towns to protest against the North America Free Trade Agreement which they thought would adversely affect the poor. When they were driven out by the Government forces, they retreated to this mountain area under the leadership of Marcos, a local hero. The owner tells me that the café stands in the middle of what is still bandit country and that Marcos and his female second-in command, who is said to be far more vicious than any of the men, are local celebrities." On one side of the café was a long shelf, full of masked bandit dolls for sale, any funds raised presumably going to support the guerrillas.

We were feeling a little apprehensive as we set off again but our coach was not held up at gunpoint and we continued safely to Agua Azul where we stopped for lunch. Agua Azul is a beauty spot noted for its many waterfalls, thundering down into what are normally deep azure blue pools, but recent heavy rain had washed down mud and silt, turning the water brown.

"We can have lunch here and you will also have time to go for a swim but please be very careful," Peter warned us. "Although this is a favourite spot for swimming, there have been many drowning accidents. There is always a strong current and undertow, which will probably be worse after the heavy rains, and there may be a lot of underwater debris. Please keep to the area indicated as safe and don't go too far from the shore."

We had two hours to spend as we wished. Neither David nor I were that keen on swimming and we decided to eat before exploring.

There were eight different restaurants, all with outside seating in the shade of thatched palm roofs, essential as the heat was now stifling. None of these looked very clean so we chose the busiest one and ordered fish from the river with bottled drinks. Afterwards we borrowed the key to the toilet. There was no running water but a bucket of water stood outside.

We then walked the short distance to the lowest waterfall which stretched across the entire width of the river, the water cascading over it at different angles. Below this, on our side of the river, was the designated swimming area. Above the first waterfall was a whole series of falls, divided by rocks into smaller cascades of varying sizes. The width of the river made the falls look much smaller in height than they actually were. We walked up the steep river bank and when we were alongside the first waterfall, we found that it was probably thirty feet high, a torrent of foaming water deflected in different directions by the underlying rocks. It looked spectacular and we felt very lucky to have seen it after the storms.

As we climbed higher, we found that the hillside had split the river into several sets of falls, tumbling down through the forest. We followed the main path and in the heat, we were soon panting from our exertions. Luckily there were a couple of benches on the way where we could sit in the shade, admire the view and recover. As we reached the upper torrents we found that these were also much higher than they had appeared from below. We could glimpse another series of falls through the trees on a different route up the hillside but our path had unfortunately come to an end, flattening out as it led to a village.

On our way back down, we stopped to admire the brilliant red, yellow and orange butterflies that were fluttering around and making the most of the spray splashing on to the banks. When they settled, they immediately closed their wings, the undersides of which resembled brown dead leaves.

There were plenty of visitors wandering up and down the path to the falls and young girls from the village were carrying baskets of tortillas and bananas which they were trying to sell, particularly to those queuing for tables in the restaurants which were now very busy. Peter had told us to be careful when walking as thefts at gunpoint had been reported at Agua Azul but, because of the number of people around, we found this difficult to believe. However, robberies may well have taken place near the more remote waterfalls that we had seen through the trees.

The two hours we had been allotted gave us ample time to have a meal and to see the falls by the main path but because we had eaten first, we had avoided the restaurant queues. The four Australians and Ian, who had all decided to go for a swim first, felt that they had been rushed. However, their verdict was that the water had been cool and refreshing and that it had been well worth the effort.

After another hour spent travelling in the coach, we stopped again, this time to visit another beauty spot, the Misol-Ha cascade. This waterfall drops thirty five metres, more than a thousand feet, into a pool in a jungle setting. It was still very hot, humid and sticky and the five swimmers immediately decided to take the opportunity for another dip. The rest of us took a footpath that led up through the jungle and round behind the falls. On the way, Peter pointed out various plants. "This is known as the "Gringo" tree," he grinned, showing us a tree with reddish papery bark, flaking off to reveal white patches underneath. "Its bark is like the skin of a white person exposed to the Mexican sun. It starts pale and then turns red and peels."

Our path wound round the side of the cliff and took us beneath an overhanging rock just behind the waterfall. Although the curtain of water was not that close, it was splashing off the rocks just below us and we were soon quite wet from the deflected spray. Looking down, we could see the five swimmers making their way along another path by the water's edge, heading towards the back of the pool. We shouted and waved to them but they were unable to hear us over the thunder of the falls.

Peter had allowed us an hour here. Once we had circled the pool, David and I walked a short distance down the road, loud with cicadas, where we found a café and sat in the cool shade sipping cold, freshly crushed orange juice. Wonderful!

When we were back on the coach, we asked our friends how they had enjoyed their swim. "We saw you walking round the lower path," I said. "The bank was too steep where we first tried to climb down to the pool," explained Cheryl, "so we had to find a place where it was easier to get to the water." "It was lovely once we were in," said Lynn. "The only problem was that the boulders around the pool were very wet and slippery with moss and algae and it was really difficult to climb out again. We all had to help each other."

From Misol-Ha, we made our way to the modern town of Palenque, only fifteen minutes drive from the Mayan ruins and built specifically to cater for the tourists. The town looked well established and had a population of about seventy thousand. We were taken to our small hotel on the outskirts of the town, where we were allocated rooms on the upper floors.

From our window, we could see that the small garden area was almost completely taken up by a very inviting swimming pool surrounded by a narrow strip of ground, on which were a few white plastic loungers plus a table and four chairs under an umbrella. The Australians and Kayleigh were soon in the water. David and I relaxed at the table with Neville and Diane, sipping cool drinks and writing a few cards. Later, the four of us walked the mile or so into town, where we found a restaurant and had an enjoyable meal together.

5

PALENQUE, YAXCHILAN, BONAMPAK AND THE MAYANS

Monday 7th July

At 8 am, we left the hotel and took a local bus to the Mayan ruins of Palenque in a lovely jungle setting. When we arrived, Peter went off to buy our tickets while we waited in a clearing near the site entrance. "Look up there," exclaimed Alan, pointing towards the trees on the far side of the clearing. Gazing up at the canopy, we saw a small troupe of monkeys leaping from one branch to another, looking as though they were playing a game of follow-my-leader. A flock of small green parakeets flew across the clearing. "Look at those," cried Lynn. "Wow," breathed Kayleigh. "I love this place."

Peter returned with a tall, slim, clean shaven man in his early forties with a dark complexion and shoulder length black hair. "This is our guide, Alphonso," he said. "We've just seen some monkeys and some green parrots," Kayleigh said excitedly to Peter. "Those monkeys are gibbons and this is part of their regular territory," Alphonso told her, smiling. "You will always see them around here. Now, if you're all ready, we'll go into the site."

We passed through the entrance gate and as we walked up the path towards the pyramids, Alphonso told us, "'Palenque,' is the modern name given to these ruins and means 'palisade'. Nobody knows what the Mayans called this ancient city. It was first occupied more than fifteen hundred years ago but it rose to prominence under a ruler known as Pakal the Great, who came to the throne in 615 AD at the age of twelve. He reigned for sixty nine years and was regarded by his people as a god. Pakal was born with a club foot, probably due to the fact that the Mayan royal family practised incest. No ordinary subject was considered worthy of them."

The centre of the site had been nearly cleared of trees, the almost flat ground being covered in very short grass as though someone had just run a lawnmower over it. The first pyramid we came to was on our left, set against a towering backdrop of trees growing up the steep hillside behind it. It had nine terraced levels with a steep stairway leading up through the centre to the temple building on top. This had five openings between broad pillars and a steep roof with a comb of separated slabs along the top edge. Although it was early, several tourists were already climbing the steps.

We joined them and from the top, looked across at a complex of buildings on a raised platform. In the centre rose a tower with a steep roof. "Over there was the site of the Royal Palace," Alphonso informed us. "The platform on which it was built measures three hundred metres by two hundred and forty metres and there are courtyards inside to provide light and space. Everything was built by manual labour without the use of animals or the wheel to transport the stones. The tower was probably used as an observatory. To the right of this complex is the highest building in Palenque, the Temple of the Inscriptions where Pakal was buried. We will visit this later."

"Palenque was deserted during the 9th century and by the time the Spaniards invaded in the 16th century, it had been almost completely buried by jungle," Alphonso went on. "You may have heard of Cortes who, having been welcomed by the Aztec king Moctezuma, deceived and killed him." We nodded. "It is said that Cortes came within forty kilometres of the ruins of Palenque as he crossed Central America but remained completely unaware of them. In the 18th century, a Spanish priest was told about the ruins by Mayan hunters and he led an expedition here and wrote a book about them. Then, in the 1830s, the Count of Waldeck, who was in his sixties at the time, lived for two years on top of one of the temples beyond the Ball Court to the north of the palace complex and, as a result, this is still known as the Temple of the Count. There were probably about five hundred buildings in this city altogether but so far, only thirty four have been excavated."

We descended the steps again and crossed to the Royal Palace complex which was reached by climbing three flights of steep steps on to the platform. "As you go round this site," suggested Alphonso, "try to imagine it all painted a rich vermilion red." The palace complex was a fascinating place with buildings linked by steps and narrow corridors with high ceilings, almost in the shape of a steep inverted V but with a narrow horizontal strip along the apex. Niches were cut into the walls and hornets were flying in and out of these darker areas where they were probably nesting. We tried not to get in their way.

In the patio where the tower stood, Alphonso pointed out sanitary installations with drains that once led to the city aqueducts. The tower itself was four storeys high, with full length openings on all four sides of the three upper storeys and with a steep-sided square flat-topped roof. "From the tower," Alphonso told us, "the sun could be observed shining directly into the Temple of the Inscriptions during the December Solstice."

The pillars and walls of the Royal Palace were once covered with fine stucco reliefs and examples of these were displayed around the site. "Mayan sculptors used a mixture of clay and tree bark," explained our guide. "This caused the stucco to dry more slowly which gave them time to carve out the reliefs in more detail. The sculptures were usually of royalty or prominent priests but they also included warriors, dancers and people offering tribute. The stucco reliefs once had jade eyes, necklaces of jade and pearls and clothing in mother-of-pearl but all these have been stolen." In one of the inner patios of the palace, the remains of stucco relief carvings could still be seen on the broad square pillars.

In the patio near the tower, we stopped to look at a stone with an oval shaped illustration etched into it. "This picture shows Sak-Kuk, the mother of Pakal, kneeling in homage to her son, the new king, and handing him the ceremonial quetzal headdress," Alphonso told us. "Although Pakal ascended to the throne at the age of nine, his mother ruled as Regent until he was considered sufficiently mature at the age of twelve to take over responsibility for the kingdom." Pakal was portrayed sitting on a couch carved with the head and legs of a jaguar at both ends and he already appeared to be wearing an extremely ornate headdress and a chain around his neck from which hung a large medallion.

Another stone tablet leaning against a wall showed Pakal wearing his quetzal feather headdress and holding a jaguar-snake, representing power and the rain-god. "Most of the temples and palaces in Palenque were constructed while Pakal was on the throne and the Royal Palace was redesigned and enlarged several times during the later years of his reign," said Alphonso. "Pakal had at least three children and on his death, his eldest son became king and completed his father's tomb. He and his brother, who succeeded him, continued to enlarge and improve the city."

In one of the patios, a row of stone slabs carved with stucco figures was lined up against the wall. Many of the figures were shown kneeling, with the left hand raised to the shoulder. "This may have been a gesture of subservience," suggested Alphonso. "There is some speculation as to whether these people were making offerings to the king or were possibly awaiting sacrifice but nobody really knows."

We now made our way to the Temple of the Sun, behind and to the right of the Royal Palace complex. Most of the pyramid was still buried under a mound but uneven ridges indicated at least nine tiers below the temple itself. On one corner, the four upper levels and a flight of steps had been exposed and renovated, leading to the temple on top. "The Temple of the Sun has the best preserved roof crest of all the temples at Palenque," said Alphonso. The airy crest was like the side of a honeycomb with four layers of openings, one above the other, rising as high again as the walls of the temple. Designs still remained visible on the steep edge of the temple roof and the broad pillars, although they were difficult to make out. "Some of the stucco decorations show offerings being made to Pakal and include descriptive hieroglyphs," clarified our guide.

"From here," he told us, "I'm going to take you on a jungle trail back to the Temple of the Inscriptions. Please don't step off the path. There are deadly bushmaster snakes in this area." "Oh, my goodness," said Diane nervously. "That's probably the reason why the grass is kept so short in the centre of the complex," her husband pointed out.

Along the trail, Alphonso showed us some termites' nests. He then broke a twig off a tree. "Pass that round and smell the sap." When Cheryl handed me the twig, I sniffed the end of it and caught an odour of TCP. "It smells like disinfectant, yes?" our guide asked, when the twig had made its way round the whole group. "This sap was used by the Mayans to cure malaria."

When we reached the Temple of the Inscriptions, Alphonso informed us, "There are sixty nine steps to the top of the Temple, one for each year of Pakal's reign. However, we have approached it from the much higher ground at the rear so you will have fewer steps to climb." We were thankful for this. However, when we reached the top of the steps, Alphonso said, "Follow me," and walked round the edge of the top platform to the front of the temple building.

The temple took up most of the platform leaving only a narrow ledge, about seventy five feet above ground level, not a place for anyone suffering from vertigo. Some of the group were very nervous and pressed against the building as they edged round but we helped each other and all made it safely. We then had a view looking down on the Royal Palace complex from above.

"This temple takes its name from the six hundred and twenty hieroglyphs carved on the inside and outside of the portico," said Alphonso. "It's the second longest text of Mayan hieroglyphs ever found. The inscriptions have not yet been completely deciphered but they record the early history of Palenque."

As well as the inscriptions, there were also some stucco reliefs. As we entered between the pillars of the portico, we saw a flight of steps leading down into the centre of the building. "It was only in 1952 that this stairway was discovered," Alphonso told us.

"This temple was constructed as the tomb of Pakal," he went on. "There are sixty nine steps down to the crypt, one for each year of Pakal's reign, the same number as on the front of the temple. Because it was built during Pakal's lifetime, a further step had to be added to the construction for every additional year the king survived. The temple building on top was added later and once had a tall roof comb above it. The crypt was discovered by an archaeologist who was excavating the staircase and found a sealed stone passageway. Inside were several skeletons, slaves buried alive to serve Pakal after death, along with tools, pottery and other items for him to use on his journey to the afterlife. Pakal's skeleton wore a jade mosaic death mask and was decorated with jewels which were taken to Mexico City, where the tomb was recreated in the National Anthropological Museum." We remembered seeing this at the start of our holiday.

"You can go down to see Pakal's burial place if you wish. The limestone lid of the sarcophagus weighs eight tons and is still down there," added our guide, describing it briefly. Nearly all of us decided to make the descent. Although electric lighting had been rigged up for visitors, the steps were very damp and slippery and there were no handrails so we took our time. At last we reached the tomb and saw the sarcophagus lid on which was engraved an image of Pakal with serpents and the Sun God and with hieroglyphs describing his reign. Alphonso had told us that figures had been etched into the wall, representing the Lords of the Underworld, but we were unable to make these out clearly in the poor lighting.

This was the first crypt discovered in any of the Mayan pyramids and at the time of our visit, nothing else so elaborate had been found. We made our way back up the steps and down the outside of the pyramid where Peter and Alphonso were waiting for us. "Your tour has now ended," said Peter "but you have a further twenty minutes to look around by yourselves, buy more water if you need it and use the public conveniences before we meet back at the entrance." This did not seem very long so we quickly thanked Alphonso and hurried off.

David and I made our way towards the north of the complex and found that the pyramids here were much smaller and had not been restored. We realised just how much work had gone into virtually rebuilding that part of the site we had already seen. Walls and steps were broken and very uneven and the Ball Court was in ruins. However, this part of the city was, in its own way, far more picturesque and atmospheric, with fine views of the remains of the buildings in their jungle setting. However, we were a little wary of the large number of hornets flying around among the trees. All too soon, our twenty minutes had elapsed and we quickly bought some water from a kiosk at the entrance as we rejoined the group.

Palenque Royal Palace complex

Corridor in Palace complex   **Temple of the Sun with roof comb**

**Steps to the Royal Palace
Yaxchilan**

**Engraving of Queen piercing
tongue**

Temple of the Sun, Yaxchilan

Early that morning, we had been given the option of taking a flight into the jungle to two more Mayan sites at Yaxchilan and Bonampak and most of us had confirmed that we would like to go. As it was so hot, Lynn and Alan had decided to spend the afternoon relaxing in the pool at the hotel. Peter had given us all maps of modern Palenque and showed them the quickest route back to the hotel before taking the rest of us on a local bus to the airport.

When we arrived, we went into the small airport building where we were each given a carrier bag containing our hot, freshly cooked packed lunch. I was already feeling a little queasy with anticipation and the smell of the hot greasy food made me feel worse but because the lunches had been brought in specifically for our group, I felt that to have refused mine would have been impolite.

Peter had booked two aeroplanes, each of which held five passengers and the pilot. The two pilots sized us up in the airport building as they needed to balance out our weights. Our pilot selected David and me, Cheryl, Sam and Diane, who was disappointed to be separated from Neville and Kayleigh. "Don't worry," said Cheryl. "We'll look after you."

The pilot took us over to his tiny plane and asked Cheryl to get in first followed by Diane. These two had to squeeze into the seats at the back. Sam, who was much larger and heavier than the rest of us, was then asked to sit in front of Cheryl who, although she was tall, was the daintiest of the group, while David sat in front of Diane. The pilot, who was slightly smaller than I was, then sat in front of Sam while I had pride of place next to the pilot. "Are you all right there, darling?" asked David from behind me.

The pilot taxied down the short runway and then we were off, flying low over the tree canopy. As we roller-coasted up and down the air pockets above the trees, I was soon turning green and was relieved that I had had the foresight to bring along the sick-bag which I had kept from our flight over from England. I made good use of this, despite being next to an open window with plenty of fresh air.

The flight took an interminable fifty minutes but at last we were descending on to a wide grassy clearing beside the Usumacinta River.

The second 'plane landed just behind us. There were some wooden benches under a canopy beside the river for us to sit and eat our picnic lunch and I made for these on wobbly legs. "You have fifteen minutes," said our pilot, "and then your guide will arrive to take you round the site."

I drank some water and after I had sat for a while, I recovered enough to eat a banana although hot, spicy chicken tacos were a little too much to cope with. Our guide then arrived, a small dark man who seemed a little lacking in confidence as he introduced himself. I wondered whether this was the first time he had led a tour group round the site.

"Welcome to Yaxchilan," he began. "My name is Enrico. This city dates back to about 200 AD and was at the height of its importance about 500 years later. It was completely buried for many years and is now being excavated from the top down."

He led us to the edge of a clearing and down through a cutting between a sloping stony wall on our left and tiers of stone on our right, similar to those we had seen in Palenque where the pyramids were still largely covered with vegetation. Facing us at the end of the cutting was a cleared vertical stone wall, about fifteen feet high, which had been one tier of a pyramid. Set back behind and above it was a further wall on which stood the remains of a roof comb although the wall looked unlike that of a temple building. To our right was another vertical wall which had been cleared of vegetation and this contained two large entrances, each with a raised stone across the threshold. We were allowed to look through these openings but not to go inside.

"Through these doorways is a maze of passages and steps leading down inside the hill," said Enrico. "We have excavated as far as we can at present but there are problems when we try to go deeper because of flooding from the Usumacinta River, which now forms part of the border between Mexico and Guatemala. The Usumacinta once divided Yaxchilan, half of which stood on the opposite bank. The river was the life-blood of the city, providing easy access for traders and pilgrims. As a result, Yaxchilan was once the major religious site in the area, rivalling Tikal and Palenque. It reached the height of its importance in the 8th century."

We left the cutting and Enrico took us to the centre of the site, a large, flat grassy oblong plaza. On one side of the plaza stood a hill, covered with trees growing through exposed rubble, while buildings had been excavated on the other three sides. One of these, a single storey building with a grass covered mound rising up just beyond its walls, had three openings in its nearest wall, spaced well apart. A two-storey building had a series of six doorways very close together on the ground floor, with further openings visible in the walls of a partially cleared upper floor and the remains of a roof-comb on top. A third building had a broad flight of steps leading up from the clearing to its single storey structure.

"Much of the information we have about Yaxchilan has come from door lintels which are now held in the Anthropological Museum in Mexico City and in the British Museum," said Enrico. "Hieroglyphs on the lintels recorded the history of the city and there were also some fine relief sculptures of the kings and their wives." As we walked round the site, we were able to go inside the ruins with their flat, grassy floors and out through openings on the opposite sides. An L-shaped top of a wall, about six foot wide, lay in the clearing in front of two of the buildings. It all looked so complete in itself that it was difficult to remember that most of the city lay buried in the ground beneath our feet.

On one side were very wide stone steps, the lowest eight steps having been cleared and apparently relaid, the upper steps still green with low vegetation and sinuously curving up and down like waves across the hillside. Above them, a narrow stone stairway led up through a clearing between the trees to the top of the hill where we caught a glimpse of a long wall with four floors of perfectly symmetrical square windows with part of a further floor of windows above. As windows were not normally part of a Mayan building, this was probably a remarkably complete roof comb with the majority of the building lying hidden under the hillside. "What you can see up there are the remains of the Royal Palace," said our guide. "We have no time to look at that today."

"Would it be all right if I run up there quickly while you continue round the site?" asked Ian. Enrico looked worried. "The steps are very uneven and some may be loose," he said doubtfully. "If you have an accident, it will be your own responsibility." "I'll come with you," Garry said to Ian. "I'd love to get a photo of the Royal Palace." The pair of them hurried up the steps while we continued round the site.

We stopped to look at the stucco engravings on some stone tablets on the lower steps and elsewhere around the site. These were far sharper and more detailed than the ones we had seen at Palenque and did not appear to be any better protected so perhaps they had been unearthed more recently. One lay flat on a low brick base abutting a path of cobblestones. "This stone has been left in the position in which it was discovered," said our guide. "It shows two kings. The one on the right who was known as Knot-Eye Jaguar ruled until the age of eighty. His son on the left was a high priest until the death of his father. He then became King Bird Jaguar and ruled until the middle of the 7th century when he was seventy. The biographical hieroglyphs in between them record the history of the two kings." Several other stone tablets bore images of kings and priests with complicated looking square hieroglyphs.

While we were looking at these, we were rejoined by Ian and Garry who were breathing heavily after racing up and down the hill. "Was it worth going up to the Royal Palace?" asked Neville. "I think I got some good photos," said Garry, "but you could see most of the building from the bottom."

Enrico now took us into one of the temples which had some clear stucco images on its walls. "Sacrificial blood was given by the Royal family and by the high priests, three people at a time," said Enrico. "This blood was provided by splitting the tongue, splitting the penis or cutting down into the tips of the fingers, all being extremely painful but not fatal. This engraving shows the Queen Regent piercing her tongue with a curved ceremonial knife. She would then have pulled a knotted rope through it. One of the lintels from the city held in the British Museum shows the spine of a stingray, for use in the bloodletting ceremony. As in other Mayan cities, ordinary subjects would have been sacrificed and given their hearts."

Enrico then took us down jungle paths to further ruins, jutting out from raised ground surrounded by trees. One of these, appropriately bathed in sunshine through a gap in the foliage, was the Temple of the Sun discovered in 1882. The little of the building that had been exposed was in an advanced state of ruin, although there was a section of high arched passageway, similar to those we had seen in the Royal Palace complex in Palenque.

As we walked through the jungle, I thought about a recent incident recounted to us by one of the guides at "Na Bolom" in San Cristobal. Only two weeks previously, an expedition sponsored by the Mexican Government had been working near the Temple of the Sun at Yaxchilan, collecting engraved stelae and artefacts for the museum in Mexico City.

"The Australian and Mexican archaeologists leading the expedition had been careful to obtain the previous permission of the local Indian tribe," the guide had told us. "Unfortunately, some of the neighbouring tribes were not so accommodating. They thought that the party of ten men, including assistants, were stealing their heritage, so they attacked them. They confiscated the men's tools and shoes, tied them to trees and beat them with machetes. They were left there to die but that night, one of them managed to break free and untied his companions. Five escaped through the jungle and five jumped into the crocodile-infested river. Only three of the five could swim so they had to support the other two. It took them between three and five days to get back to civilisation but miraculously, all ten survived." Diane had also heard this story, which had been reported in Time magazine in an article entitled "The Great Escape". She had purchased a copy of the magazine in San Cristobal and had passed it round the group for us all to read.

It was now time for us to return to the aircraft. "Before we go, are there any toilet facilities on site?" I asked our pilot. He grinned and pointed to the nearby bushes. "I'll come with you," said Diane. Cheryl joined us and behind the bushes, we found a small clearing and checked carefully for snakes and spiders. All we found was a very large toad that silently sat and watched us. A few moments later, we were back on board the aeroplane and taking off over the Usumacinta River.

The flight to Bonampak only took twenty minutes and despite my misgivings, I managed to survive the journey without being ill. The pilot pointed out the runway to me, a narrow strip of lighter green cut between the trees in the middle of thousands of acres of jungle. The aeroplanes were very old with the most primitive of instruments and our pilot used only his own knowledge of the lie of the land to guide him to this particular spot.

The landing was very exciting as the landing strip was not much wider than the wingspan of the aircraft. We came in low over the trees, gently eased between them and touched down safely on the grass, where we bounced along on the uneven ground to a wider turning circle at the end of the landing strip. The other aeroplane had landed first and had already turned to face back up the runway again.

There were no guides to show us around Bonampak and we had an hour to explore by ourselves. Before we had left Palenque, Peter had given each of us an information sheet. This told us that the city was only discovered in 1946 although the local Lacandon Indians, descendants of the Mayans, still worshipped at the ancient temples.

At one end of the central grassed plaza area, broad stone steps covered the side of a hill. About halfway up the hill was the building known as the Temple of the Frescoes for which Bonampak is known. David and I climbed up there first. We found that the walls inside the Temple were covered by three huge painted murals. A guard stood by to ensure that nobody attempted to take photographs.

The lighting inside the building was poor but it was possible to make out three scenes. The first showed the preparations for battle, with the king consulting his advisors and musicians playing in the background; the second showed the battle itself and the capture of hostages who would probably be sacrificed; while the final mural showed the victory celebrations and ritual bloodletting. These paintings alone made the visit worthwhile.

Our information sheet told us that the 8th century frescoes had no joins in the plaster, indicating that each room had been painted in a single session before the stucco dried. At some time, water had seeped through the roof plaster, coating the paintings with a layer of semi-transparent calcium carbonate which had preserved them from further damage.

When we came out, David and I climbed the steps to the top of the hill, where there were several small ruined temples. Some were fairly solid structures, one or two storeys high with door and window openings, but one had five walls lying parallel to each other, partially roofed over with stones. Between the walls, we could see the jungle. There were wonderful views from up here across the vast canopy of the Lacandon rainforest with its many different shades of green.

As we came down again, we looked at two stelae carved with stucco designs which stood on the lower steps, each protected by a perspex cover on four poles. The first stone was undamaged and showed a king in the centre dressed in a tunic, boots and fringed socks who appeared to be wearing a necklace with a human head dangling from a chain down his back. He towered over a woman standing behind him and another person standing in front, possibly his queen and his son as all three were wearing very tall and elaborate headdresses.

The second stone had been pieced together and apparently showed the king looking down on a captive kneeling before him who was pleading for his life. Above the king was what may have been a jaguar-quetzal god, half the height of the king himself.

Two further stelae stood in the flat plaza area, the larger one again protected by a perspex cover. This stone was also pieced together but appeared to show a king or high priest holding a decorative sword or sceptre of state, reaching from the ground to chest height and embellished with various ornaments down the length of its blade or sheath. We were sorry that there was no guide here to interpret the carvings and tell us the stories behind the various stelae.

Trees were scattered across the plaza and as I watched, a lizard about two feet long scuttled for cover in the undergrowth. The jungle seemed much closer here than at Yaxchilan and although the ruins of Bonampak were less impressive than others we had seen, they blended in with the more wooded site. The only person we saw apart from our group was the guard in the Temple of the Frescoes and it felt a very peaceful place.

By the time we had spent an hour here, it was beginning to spot with rain and the other pilot was urging his five passengers back into the aircraft. They were the first to leave and as the rest of us reached the end of the landing strip nearest to the site, their aeroplane came speeding towards us along the grass and took off over our heads.

It was then our turn to take off for the thirty five minute flight back to Palenque. As we flew into a rain cloud, we could tell why the pilots had wanted us to hurry. The rain completely blotted out the view through the cockpit windscreen and there were no wipers to clear it. On the way back, the pilot had to drop down to where the cloud thinned and lean out of the side window to get his bearings before climbing again. I guessed that the turbulence made it too dangerous to risk flying low over the tree canopy, as we had on the way out to Yaxchilan.

As we neared the airport, the pilot took out his mobile telephone and was talked down until we dropped below cloud level again. Although it was still raining, we could now see the runway and we landed safely. Peter met us in the airport building and we took a bus back into town, passing a large white sculptured Mayan head in the centre of a roundabout as we entered the modern town of Palenque.

That evening, the rain had stopped and Peter took us all to a restaurant at the far end of town. Here, they had set up a long table for us outside, where we caught a cooling breeze. David chose a pork dish while I had fish. There were some unusual drinks on the menu and I tried a papaya con leché, papaya blended with milk. This was served in an enormous brandy glass, filled to the brim and it was thick, smooth and delicious.

Tuesday 8th July

We were up early and after a cool, refreshing shower, we had a light breakfast on the first floor terrace overlooking the pool. Although it was only 7am, the sun was already hot enough to burn our skin. We then packed all the luggage and ourselves into the two combis that were waiting outside the hotel and set off on a very cramped journey towards Guatemala.

The road gradually deteriorated from a good tarmac surface near Palenque to tarmac with potholes. The patches of tarmac then gradually decreased until we were driving on a dirt road. We passed through an area known for its iguanas and when our drivers spotted some, they stopped the combis so we could climb out for a better look. Beside the road grew shrubs with long sprays of white blossoms amongst which flitted some beautiful butterflies, the upper half of their wings banded with broad deep orange and narrow dark brown stripes, the lower half in stripes of brown and cream.

"I can't see any iguanas," said Kayleigh, peering up into the trees. "Look up there at that gap in the foliage," said Peter, pointing. "There's a bare branch with an iguana along the top. See it?" "Hey, neat."

The iguanas were very well camouflaged and until they moved, they were difficult to detect in the combination of light and shadow up in the trees. They were probably eight to ten feet long, more than half this length being taken up by their tails, and were almost the exact shade of the tree bark on which they sat but with pronounced spines along their backs and dark banding on their tails. Once we had seen one, it was easier to spot more.

"What's happening up there?" asked Sue. A large bird was flapping and making pecking motions at one of the iguanas, making gallant efforts to scare it away, but the iguana continued to advance very slowly and determinedly along the branch. "That bird's a vulture," said our driver, who spoke excellent English. "It looks as though the iguana has discovered its nest and is after its eggs."

We returned to the combis and continued on our way until 11.30 am, when we stopped in a small town outside a supermarket. "You have twenty minutes here," said Peter. "You will need to buy yourself something for a packed lunch. Also, this is the last chance to spend your Mexican pesos so make sure you use up all your loose change."

We wandered around the supermarket, looking at all the options and comparing prices. Once we had bought enough for a picnic, David and I spent the rest of our change on a couple of bottles of sugar cane liqueur.

When we had got out of the combi to look at the iguanas, we had all changed seats as we got back in. We now changed seats again. This gave everybody a turn to sit in the slightly less cramped seats at the front. It was now my turn with Ian and the view was so much better. "Look," I said, "That looks like a tortoise at the side of the road." "It's a turtle," said our driver. A few miles further on, Ian said, "There's a monitor lizard." "Where?" "There, just coming out of that ditch at the side of the road." The driver slowed and the monitor lizard crossed the road right in front of us. "Jeez, look at that" said Garry who was sitting just behind us. "It's enormous." It must have been at least five feet long from its head to the tip of its tail.

We were now driving along a sandy track through flat sugar cane country with a range of mountains in the distance. We passed several carts looking like shaggy moving haystacks, piled high with, and almost completely hidden by, newly cut canes which hung over the sides and backs of the carts almost down to the ground. After a further hour, we reached the port of La Palma on the San Pedro River.

The combis pulled up near a bridge that looked as though it was constructed from metal pipes of varying diameters. We unloaded the luggage and carried our cases about fifty yards to a large, square roof canopy supported by four concrete corner posts, adjacent to a flight of steps leading down to the river. Plastic tables and chairs had been arranged under the canopy and we were able to sit and eat our picnics in comfort in the shade. Much to everybody's relief, there was a café nearby with toilets which we were allowed to use.

After a while, two long, narrow motorised boats arrived to take us up-river. They each had an uncovered area at the front for luggage and an awning over seven individual passenger seats. We humped our own bags down the steps and these were loaded into the front of the boats first. We then had to climb over the luggage to get to our chairs, arranged two abreast with one at the back. Peter, Cheryl and Sam, Lynn and Alan, Garry and Ian got into the first boat. David and I, Neville and Diane, Kayleigh and Sue climbed on board the second boat where a single passenger was already occupying the seat at the rear.

The chairs were moveable and wooden but the seats had been hollowed out into a shape rather like that of the canvas of an old-fashioned deck-chair, so we sank into them rather than perching on top. Once we were settled, the motors were started and we began a four hour boat trip up the San Pedro River. The wooden seats were quite comfortable at first but we found them very hard before the end of the journey.

Shortly after we set off, we passed herds of hump-backed zebu cattle grazing on open ground near the river bank but it was not long before we entered the rainforest. Apart from herons and cormorants, there was little wildlife to be seen but the river itself was wonderful. It split up into narrow channels, the forest growing right to the water's edge and the canopy meeting overhead in places, so that we appeared to be heading into tunnels among the trees before the channels joined and widened out again.

The crew had to know the river as we motored past submerged tree trunks. In places, we saw rocks just beneath the surface, skimming across them at their lowest point. If the water level had dropped any further, parts of the river would have been unnavigable. Once or twice we entered what appeared to be a narrow arm of the river finishing in a dead end but then we turned into a sharp bend, hidden by vegetation, and joined the main river again.

As we circumnavigated a line of rocks that jutted above water level and spanned half the width of the river, we noticed the sky beginning to darken. The crew quickly covered the luggage with a tarpaulin as

113

the sky turned black and we were suddenly caught in a tropical storm. The wind was blowing the rain sideways into the boat, along the side where I was sitting. It was too hot to wear waterproofs but several of us had umbrellas so those of us along that side formed a wall of umbrellas and cowered behind them. In minutes, the floor of the boat was running with water and we hoped that the luggage at the bottom of the pile was waterproof. Luckily, the downpour only lasted fifteen minutes.

Shortly after the rain had ceased, we stopped in mid-river to allow our non-Explore passenger to transfer to a waiting dugout canoe, in order to continue his journey. This passenger only had a small overnight bag and as soon as he was seated aboard the canoe, the two oarsmen started rowing and they sped away down a side tributary of the San Pedro. We waited until they were well clear before we continued upstream.

The next bit of excitement came when the width of the river was suddenly compressed into a narrow waterfall, nearly a foot high, with a huge volume of water gushing over it. The other boat was in front of us and our skipper pulled over to one side. As we watched, the engine of the other boat revved and it raced towards the waterfall. The bow lifted as it rose up the fall but the boat stuck halfway, then gradually slid back again.

Peter was on that boat and suggested to the Australians, Garry and Ian that they should move to the stern of the boat to tip up the bow. The boat rushed at the waterfall again and as it started to go over, everybody ran towards the bow which was already weighted down with the luggage. This brought the stern up so the boat slid smoothly across and once they were seated again, Cheryl and Sam, who were near the back just in front of Peter, turned round and gave us the 'thumbs up'. We now knew what to do and managed to cross the waterfall at the first attempt.

Further on, we came to another waterfall but this was wider with slightly less depth of water gushing over it and the crew made us all get out to lighten the weight while they took the boat through. This was clearly a regular occurrence because a footpath had been trodden out around this section of the river and having walked a short distance past the waterfall, we climbed back on board. It had been good to stretch our legs for a few minutes.

After travelling for two and a half hours, we reached the Mexican Customs and the boats were moored. Peter collected all our passports and Mexican exit forms and took them to the Customs House. While we waited, we fed the river fish with biscuits left over from lunch – they were voracious. Lynn and Alan recognised some of the fish and pointed out gouramis up to four inches long, striped tiger barbs and guppies. This kept us amused until Peter returned and we set off again. A short distance further on, we crossed the border, marked by a line of white posts looking like trig points, stretching from the river up into the hills on either side.

Half an hour later, we approached a village and I took a photograph before realising we had reached the Guatemalan Customs where photographs were forbidden. Nobody seemed to have noticed, however. Once again we moored and Peter took all our passports to the Customs Office while we fed the fish. After we set off once more, we only had to travel upriver for a further half hour or so before reaching our destination, a jungle lodge.

There was a landing stage on the left side of the river where the boats were moored and the crew unloaded the luggage. We found our own cases and carried them up a flight of wooden steps and between the trees to the Reception building which was also the restaurant and consisted of a large platform on stilts. On the right was the restaurant area, with a low bamboo perimeter wall and four corner beams. These supported a high palm leaf canopy which shaded the wooden tables and benches and provided shelter from the rain. On the left was the Reception/kitchen with its own canopy, where meals were cooked over an open fire and bottled soft drinks could be purchased over the counter. The two areas were separated by steps leading up to the platform on either side.

We sat at the tables while Peter obtained and handed out the keys to the cabins. "When you've got rid of your cases, I'll see you back here," he said. The cabins were uphill from the Reception area, grouped together along one edge of a small clearing. These were very attractive rustic bamboo huts with thick shaggy roofs, possibly made of sugar cane leaves. Inside, six foot high partitions separated the rooms with space above to allow the air to circulate and there was also space between the roof and the outer walls. David and I took our luggage into our room and found a small compartment at the back of the cabin, containing a toilet and washbasin but with no water. Over each bed was a rolled-up mosquito net suspended from a roof beam.

"I suggest we spread our nets out around our beds and spray them in case there are any mosquitoes lurking inside," said David. "That will give the fumes a chance to disperse while we are out of the room." "That's a good idea," I agreed, delving in my rucksack for the insect spray. "I'll find the torches as well. We'll probably need them to make our way back to the cabin."

By the time we were ready, the camp was being lashed by another tropical storm so we armed ourselves with the torches and umbrellas and made our way back to the Reception area to join the rest of the group. They had already pushed the tables together to make one long table and we sat around this on the benches, chatting over the drinks which we bought from the kitchen. Darkness fell early but a generator provided light for three bulbs, two suspended on cords over the table and one in the kitchen area.

Over the open fire, two women cooks rustled up an amazing banquet of chicken, chips, carrots and another unidentified vegetable. After the meal, David passed round our two bottles of cane sugar liqueur, which tasted like raw alcohol, while we sat and talked and tried to avoid the insects attracted by the lights.

One enormous insect was like a rounded dragonfly. Kayleigh shrieked when it came near her. "Just ignore it," her father told her. "It won't hurt you if you leave it alone." Shortly afterwards, it stung him on the neck and he swore, slapped at it and flattened it. "Are you all right, Nev?" asked Diane, concerned. Kayleigh just grinned wickedly. "So much for leaving it alone," she said, her voice dripping with sarcasm.

During the evening, after the rain had stopped, Sue went to collect something from her cabin and came back a few minutes later. "Do go up there and look at the fireflies," she said. We wandered up into the clearing away from the lights. Ian had been using his torch to see where he was walking. "Turn your torch off," Garry said to him. We stood there gazing into the darkness and were enchanted. There were millions of fireflies, pale green lights twinkling in the trees around the clearing and down by the river. It was a magical sight.

Before we returned to our cabins for the night, Peter warned us, "Please remember to shake out your shoes before you put them on in the morning. There could be a spider or scorpion hiding inside." Back in our room, David and I took off our shoes but otherwise decided to lie on our beds fully dressed, each with a bottle of water and a torch. We tucked our mosquito nets round the edges of our mattresses, put out the torches and lay there in our individual netting tents, listening to the noises of the night and whispering to each other, "What was that?" From time to time we used a torch to try to identify the source of a particular noise.

A gecko ran around the framework of the roof, squeaking excitedly whenever it caught something and making loud kissing noises from time to time. Then we were visited by a pair of coati mundis that had climbed over the six foot outer wall and were trying to get into our cases, which were fortunately still locked. Not having any success, they then climbed over into the adjacent bedroom where Neville and Diane were trying to sleep. Here they had more luck as they found a carrier bag containing the remains of the picnic lunches. We could hear our friends muttering to each other, "What's that?" and we saw their torches flashing. The coati mundis made so much noise that, in desperation, Neville braved the mosquitoes and any other insects that may have made their way into the cabin and put the carrier bag outside the door. Eventually we all managed to get some sleep.

Wednesday 9th July

The next morning, I was woken by a fearsome roaring noise at 5am. It sounded like a pride of lions but I knew from experience that it was only howler monkeys. It was getting light so I decided to see if I could spot any early morning wildlife outside. Holding my boots upright, I tapped the heels sharply on the floor, carefully checking them for spiders or scorpions before putting them on. In the bathroom area, I used a little of the precious drinking water out of my bottle to rinse my face and clean my teeth. I then felt ready to face the day.

Leaving David asleep in bed, I quietly stepped out of the cabin and found chickens scuttling across the clearing. As I walked around the edge of the forest, a young boy aged about twelve came down a footpath and beckoned to me to follow him. He led me a short way into the jungle and pointed high up into the tree canopy where I could see three howler monkeys moving about through the branches.

My new friend spoke very little English but indicated that he came from a nearby village and that his name was Luis. I spotted an orange furry creature vanishing into the undergrowth but Luis was unable to tell me what it was in English and the Spanish name meant nothing to me. I then saw a squirrel. After this, Luis and I walked down to the river which was very still and peaceful in the early morning light, with clear reflections of the trees on the opposite bank. By this time the rest of the group were beginning to emerge from their cabins.

When I saw David, he had a rash of red spots across his throat. "What's happened to your neck, darling? It looks as though you've been bitten." Diane took a close look. "Those are ant bites," she said. "Your bed must have been placed over an ant run." "I'm surprised the ants didn't keep you awake," I said. "Those bites look very itchy. I'll go and get the anti-histamine cream."

I went to the cabin and when I returned, David and Diane were talking about the coati mundis. "When I lived in Indonesia, we were always getting them in the bedroom," she was saying. "They are very curious creatures. I wore some dangly earrings in bed one night and

Rainforest accommodation

Early morning view of the San Pedro River

Guatemalan village

Meeting the children

I was woken up by one of them batting at an earring with its paw to see how it reflected the light." We were laughing as we made our way to the table for breakfast.

The kitchen fire had been alight for some time and the cooks came up with another wonderful meal, this time consisting of scrambled egg containing chopped green peppers with fried plantains and what looked like chocolate sauce but was made of black beans. We had coffee and orange juice to drink. After breakfast, Peter told us, "The water will be turned on for five minutes so you can flush the toilets and wash your hands." "Hey, luxury!" said Garry. "That's one flush per cabin, not per person" Peter clarified.

At 6.30 am, half a dozen school children, including Luis, arrived from the nearby village with their school satchels on their backs. Luis waved as he saw me. They made their way down the bank to a dugout canoe and paddled themselves across the river to go to school. About half an hour after that, we had loaded all the luggage into the bows of our two boats and clambered aboard. We then set off for El Naranjo in the Peten region of Guatemala, only five minutes upstream but on the opposite bank of the San Pedro River.

6

GUATEMALA

At El Naranjo, the boats were run ashore on to a gently sloping beach of mud and pebbles, so that we could climb over the luggage on to dry land. The luggage was then unloaded and we carried it a little way up the slope from the river and waited for our next transport to arrive. A pig with large black spots and very long legs was wandering across the stony mud looking unsuccessfully for something to eat, as there was not a single blade of grass here.

At the top of the slope were some wooden shacks, open at the front, with corrugated iron roofs supported by poles. Although the shack on the far left was some distance away, we could see joints of meat strung up from the front edge of its roof. This probably belonged to the village butcher, along with the pig.

It was not long before our coach arrived. The driver began reversing down the slope towards the river to make it easier to load up the luggage. Unfortunately, when he stopped the engine, the coach continued to slide backwards on the mud, heading slowly but relentlessly towards the river. "Quickly," said Peter. "Bring me some stones." He grabbed a couple of the larger pebbles and risked life and limb to place them just behind the back wheels of the coach. As we envisaged our transport being marooned in the San Pedro River, we all rushed around collecting pebbles which Peter and Garry piled up behind the wheels of the coach until it was stationary.

Luckily, once the engine was started, the coach had sufficient purchase to get back up the slope and we walked up behind it with the cases. The luggage was soon loaded and once we were all on board, we set off to explore Guatemala. This was a lovely rural country of stone and gravel roads cutting through lush green wooded hills. Village houses were roofed in corrugated iron or thatch and nestled among the trees.

After an hour and a half, we stopped on the outskirts of a village where Peter had arranged for us to visit the school. The village was built on a hill and as we wandered down the centre of the deserted gravel road, we looked down on the tree canopy in the valley to our right and towards hills in the distance. Compared to El Naranjo, this village looked quite prosperous and very picturesque.

The houses were built of timber with reed-thatched roofs and open doors although several had no windows. Some of the properties had land fenced off around them where the owners grew banana palms and other crops. A few even had flowering trees and shrubs with smaller flowering plants growing in containers. Here and there, we saw hens or a horse and behind a couple of houses, a line of washing had been hung out to dry. Everywhere looked clean and neat with no sign of any litter.

We walked past some stalls laden with fruit and vegetables and a wooden building that was the pharmacy, according to a large sign on the wire perimeter fence. Further on was the village pond, covered in floating green duckweed, where a woman was collecting water in a bucket and six white geese with orange-yellow beaks were swimming happily. I wondered whether this was the only water supply for the village but Peter was some way ahead and later I forgot to ask.

Children in Guatemala attend school between the ages of seven and thirteen but younger children came out of their homes to watch us go by and the bolder ones came into the road to greet us. They were generally barefoot but otherwise neatly dressed. A teenage girl rode past on a bicycle and shyly smiled.

When we reached the school, there was great excitement. This was Peter's first visit here but Explore groups had visited this school on earlier tours and he had brought with him some photographs of the children, taken by the previous tour leader. He handed these to one of the teachers and we expected the children to rush over to look at them but they were well disciplined and stayed where they were.

The school was divided into two classrooms where children were learning in mixed age groups. Each room held five long tables, with up to four children sitting at each table, facing the teacher at the front. As we wandered around looking at the children's work, saying "bueno" to everyone and making sure no child was overlooked, we quickly discovered that all the children were learning different subjects. It seemed that once the children had learnt to read, they could choose what they wanted to learn from the books available, progressing at their own speed with the teacher acting as a facilitator, giving help and advice as required. David wrote down some simple sums for those learning arithmetic and found that the children had no problem with basic addition, subtraction, multiplication or division.

We left our gifts with the two teachers who told David and me that our pencils from the market in San Cristobal were greatly appreciated, as there was always a shortage of writing materials. To thank us for the gifts and photographs, one of the classes then sang for us. It was delightful and we all applauded and whooped as loudly as we could.

The upper part of one wall of the school was made of chicken wire to let in light and air and while we were in the classrooms, the younger children pressed up against this wall, peering at us through the wire. As soon as we stepped outside again, these youngsters began begging us to take their photographs, hoping that theirs would be among those delivered to the village by a future tour group.

One young mother proudly brought out her two daughters. The toddler was dressed in her best party frock of red silk with a froth of white lace around the hem, with matching red socks and white lace-up shoes, while her big sister, aged about four, wore a pale yellow lacy party dress with pink socks and black shoes. The mother had obviously dressed them up for the occasion. When she insisted that I took a photograph of them, I did not have the heart to refuse although I preferred the children acting naturally in their everyday wear. They were all very attractive with dark hair and eyes, coffee coloured skin and cheeky grins. As we walked back through the village, children stood in little groups trying to catch our attention but regrettably, we each had only a limited supply of film and it was not possible to photograph all of them. Eventually we rejoined the coach and set off again.

We had been travelling for about an hour when the coach suddenly swerved off the road into the bushes and then back on to the road again before stopping. The driver got out. "What's happened?" queried Sue. "I don't know," said Peter. "I'll find out." As the passengers on one side of the coach brushed off the leaves, twigs and insects that had swept in on them through the open windows, we wondered briefly if the driver had fallen asleep at the wheel. We were doing him an injustice, however, as the cause of our swerve had been a burst tyre.

The driver was carrying a spare and we all got off the coach and wandered along the roadside while the tyre was being changed. This time, there were no other vehicles on the road and our driver had to manage single-handedly, although Peter did offer his help, which was refused. We passed the time looking at the red and green bromeliads which grew along the otherwise bare branches of dead trees and at a myriad of very tiny butterflies on the wild flowers growing on either side of the road. Howler monkeys were roaring in the distance.

Once the tyre was replaced, we returned to the coach and after picking the rest of the twigs and leaves off the seats and putting them out of the window, we were soon on our way once more. After a further hour's travelling, we reached the village of San Diego where another school visit had been arranged. Again the coach was parked at one end of the village and we walked down to the school.

In this village, wooden houses were erected in clearings in the forest rather than in fenced gardens and some were roofed with corrugated iron rather than thatch. Although the corrugated iron may have been more efficient at keeping out the rain, it made the village a little less picturesque. A broad side path of grass and clay led down the hill between the houses and trees to a river or lake in the valley and everywhere was again clean, tidy and litter-free.

The school here had four classrooms. In one of these, an art class was in full swing, the children making their own designs using brightly coloured poster paints. In each of the other classrooms, the children were studying a variety of subjects including reading, writing, arithmetic, geography and botany. As in the previous school, there appeared to be a mixed age range in each class. We again tried to ensure that no child was overlooked and spoke to everybody as we went round the classrooms admiring the work.

We had arrived just before the lunch break. David noticed a bucket of liquid in one of the classrooms and when he asked the teacher what it was, she explained that it contained soup for the children's lunch. It looked like starvation rations but the children appeared to be very healthy and we decided they must eat reasonably well at home. We all left our gifts with the teachers and on this occasion, David and I gave the packets of mixed fruit and nuts and the balloons, which were received with smiles and thanks.

As we left the building, the children followed us out, begging to have their photographs taken. They were so anxious that they pressed up too closely for this to be possible. "Sit," I said, making a downward hand movement and as some of the front ones went down on their knees, "Bueno. Stay." I then backed hurriedly until I could get a group of them in the viewfinder and quickly took a photograph before more children rushed in front of them. David helped to control them and I took several group photographs of the children, copies of which we later sent to Explore to be passed on to the school by a later tour group.

Peter now took us to the village restaurant for lunch. We walked into an enclosed room, half of which was taken up by clay ovens with blazing fires inside. The heat was stifling. We were offered a choice of soup, tortillas, rice, chicken and beans. "I don't really feel hungry," I said to David. "I think I'll just have a cold drink." "It's too hot for a cooked meal," he agreed. "There's a refrigerator over there. Let's see what they have." Inside we found sealed plastic tubes of chilled fresh orange juice. We bought one each and hurried outside into the fresh air where the heat of the midday sun was far more bearable. The juice was refreshing, cold and delicious and just what we needed.

From here, we had a coach journey of a further two and a half hours, during which time the road surface deteriorated rapidly. In one place, the road had collapsed completely and had obviously been in this state for a considerable length of time as a lily pond had developed between the broken edges of the road. We could just see it as we skirted round a track through the forest, the driver edging the coach between the trees to get back on to the road.

The driver tried to avoid the worst of the potholes in the centre of the road by keeping as far over to the side as possible but at times, as the outer wheels left the road, the coach tilted at angles of up to 45° and we clung on tightly to the seats in front, wondering whether it would topple over. However, we safely reached beautiful Lake Peten Itza and across the lake, we could see the causeway to Flores, the capital of the Peten region, which was built on an island.

"Cortes and his conquistadores first visited Flores in the early 16th century and for some reason, they treated the Indians well," Peter told us. "When they left, they abandoned a lame donkey. The Indians thought the donkey was a gift and fed it the best food they had. When it died, they made a statue of it and worshipped it as a god. However, the Spaniards returned at the end of the 17th century and completely destroyed the town. The present town of Flores was built on its ruins."

Our hotel stood on the lake shore in the mainland town of Santa Elena and was clean and modern with attractive thatched roofs. We were now free for the rest of the day. "I'd like to see Flores but first, if you don't mind, I need to have a shower, wash my hair and change my clothes," I said. "I know what you mean," agreed David. "Having worn these things overnight, I feel like a tramp." It was not long before we were feeling clean and fresh again and we set off on foot to explore Flores. About a mile from the hotel, we caught a bus to take us over the causeway.

When we arrived, we found a pleasant small town built on a hill, with steep roads leading down to the lake in all directions. At the top of the hill was the main square, in the centre of which was a small park with ornamental palms and an enormous flame tree, its branches covered with bright red flowers. There was also a large stone carved with Mayan designs which looked as though it was the upper part of a stele from one of the archaeological sites. Some children were playing hide and seek and peeped out at us between the trees, laughing.

On one side of the square stood the white Cathedral which had two large bell towers and a very small clock in the centre top of the main façade. On its right were the Government offices, a two storey whitewashed building with an upstairs balcony and curtains up at the windows, giving the appearance of residential accommodation. Across the square was the museum which was promoting local Indian crafts.

We went into the museum to get out of the sun and cool down. On one side of the entrance hall was a shop selling good quality wooden carvings and we spent some time here being tempted by various items. We eventually chose a hinged container shaped like a shell, in a dark polished wood with beautiful graining, to give as a Christmas present to one of our friends.

Just downhill from the main square was a single storey cream building with three doors above which, respectively, were the signs "Banda", "Civil" and "Departmental" in large brown lettering. Outside, about twenty bicycles were propped against the wall and each other. These belonged to members of the town band who were inside, busily practising. As we were walking past, we stopped to listen and decided, on balance, that the band members were probably all attempting to play the same tune but in several different keys. They clearly needed a conductor as the timing also left something to be desired, so it sounded horrendous. Still, they were enjoying themselves and seemed quite pleased with the results, because they were laughing and joking beside the open windows as they rested between pieces.

We explored the streets on all sides of the island. The steep roads were cobbled and the one or two storey buildings were plastered and mostly painted in delicate pastel shades although some were in deeper hues. The roofs of wood or corrugated iron were all painted red so the scene looked very picturesque, particularly with the blue sky reflected in the lake with the wooded shore beyond.

The heat was making us thirsty so we found a café selling cold drinks and sat inside for a while, sipping fruit juices and cooling down. Eventually we made our way back to the quay and bus stop. We missed the first bus due to a misunderstanding. It came over the causeway and stopped for people to get off. We thought it would turn round and wait for passengers or perhaps even circle the island before returning to the mainland. However, it turned round and went straight back over the causeway without stopping again. We took the next bus which dropped us outside the hotel.

Although the hotel Reception and our bedrooms were in a building on the lake shore, the restaurant and swimming pool were on their own little island, surrounded by patches of water lilies and water hyacinths floating on the surface of the lake. The edge of the island was walled round with stone so we thought it may have been artificial but it looked very attractive. The buildings, which were largely open, had pink plaster walls and high pointed reed-thatched roofs and they stood in a small grassy garden, where thatched parasols and sun loungers were arranged around the pool.

This island was reached by an angled walkway over the water, patched up with planks of wood where the original wooden slats had rotted through. We crossed to the restaurant and while we were sitting waiting for our meal to arrive, the last rays of the setting sun were reflected in gold across the darkening lake.

Later that night, we played card games with our friends until the restaurant lights went out and it was time to make our way back across the causeway. "I forgot to bring the torches," I said. "So did I," said Cheryl. "Did anyone bring a torch?" Nobody had thought about it and the lights in the main part of the hotel were on the far side, facing the road. In almost total darkness, we edged to the start of the walkway and, giggling, felt our way across. It was quite exciting.

Thursday 10th July

The next morning, we were leaving Flores and had our cases packed and ready early. After breakfast, we were joined by our guide for the day, Lucas from Nicaragua. We were provided with a luxury coach, quite a change from the one on the previous day and having loaded the luggage, set off in comfort for Tikal.

As we drove along the shore of Lake Peten Itza, Lucas told us, "The word 'peten' means 'island'. Flores was founded by a Mayan tribe called the Itzas who originated from Chichen Itza in Yucatan. It was Peten Itza, the island of the Itza tribe, that gave its name to the lake."

We had only been travelling for a few minutes when we stopped beside the lake near a row of craft stalls. "The Government is trying to stop the Indians using the traditional slash and burn method to clear the land for crops," Lucas told us. "Instead, they are encouraging them to make money from crafts. A mahogany tree would once have been burnt in a few hours as firewood for cooking but now a single tree will last a family for a year in the form of carvings. To make this policy work, however, tourists must buy."

As well as woodcarvings, there were stalls with an array of woven and embroidered materials in a huge variety of colours and designs. They were beautiful but expensive compared to similar goods we had seen in Mexico. However, we were all tempted by something. Most of the others bought a selection of textiles while David and I fell in love with and purchased a delicately carved wooden scorpion in shades of dark brown and tan with eight bent, jointed legs, a pair of jointed threatening pincers and a wicked looking curved and jointed tail.

As we set off again, Lucas informed us that Flores was sinking while at the same time, the level of the lake was rising. "In 1969, the lake rose by four metres and parts of Flores are already under water," he said. "The first floor of the hotel where you were staying is now completely submerged." The owners had clearly done an excellent job of moving everything up to its present level, as we would never have guessed.

Flores across Lake Peten Itza

Hotel restaurant, Lake Peten Itza

Valerie Astill

Temple of the Great Jaguar, Tikal   **Temple of the Masks, Tikal**

Central Plaza, Temple of the Great Jaguar and steps to the Northern Acropolis
(Chensiyuan, Wikimedia Commons)

Lucas started telling us about the flora and fauna around the lake. "Lake Peten Itza supports twenty four different kinds of fish but it is best known for its white bass." I had seen bass on the restaurant menu the previous evening and now wished I had tried it. Lucas also told us that the area was noted for the richness of its wildlife including crocodiles, various kinds of monkeys, jaguars, pumas and a wide variety of birds.

We reached the Mayan site of Tikal and as we walked from the coach park to the entrance, Lucas pointed out some howler monkeys, leaping through the tree canopy on the edge of a clearing. He also showed us a large cicada on the path, the first time I had actually seen one although I had heard them often enough. It was similar in shape to a grasshopper, although its body looked shorter and broader at the front and it was jet black in colour.

There was a board at the entrance to Tikal with a map of the site. Lucas stopped us here to explain that the city had originally extended across thirty six square kilometres in nine different complexes. "Every twenty years," he told us, "a ruler was elected or re-elected for the next twenty years. The succession usually passed from father to son and a new complex was built for each ruler."

From the entrance, we followed a stony path which led fairly steeply uphill through the jungle. As we climbed, Lucas kept stopping to show us various plants which gave us a chance to keep together and catch our breath. Pausing beside one tree, he told us, "This is the sapodilla tree, a relative of the rubber tree. At the time of the full moon, V-shaped cuts are made in the trunk and gravity makes the sap run out. The sap is collected, cooked and exported for chewing gum. The Mayans used the wood of the sapodilla for lintels as it is hard and very strong. They also used the wood for cooking as it is fibrous and makes a better fuel than coal."

Further along the jungle path, Lucas showed us the type of liana that the Indians cut for drinking water. "Do I have a volunteer to taste it?" he asked. Ian bravely stepped forward. "I will," he said. Lucas cut the vine with his knife and a clear liquid ran out. Ian held it above his head and let the liquid trickle into his mouth while we waited expectantly. "It tastes just like ordinary water," was the verdict.

We then came to an enormous tree that Lucas told us was a ceiba. "This is a softwood that the Indians use for dugout canoes." Of another tree he said, "This is the copal or incense tree, used in Mayan ceremonies. Incidentally," he added, "like the Mayans, local Indians still time many of their everyday activities, such as having a haircut, according to the phases of the Moon."

By this time, the path had levelled out and we came to the first of the pyramids. A flight of seven steps led up between the walls of the bottom tier which was constructed from six rows of smooth stone blocks with the second and fourth layers standing proud, the inset row between them being decorated with circles in relief. The fifth row was again set back and engraved with a repeat design resembling the splayed lower half of a harvested stook of corn and, rather than being vertical, this and the sixth row together curved outwards, widening the base of the first platform.

There was only time for a quick photograph, as Lucas continued walking past the pyramid towards the Central Acropolis. As we entered the main part of the ruins, Lucas asked us to try to imagine the city in its former glory. "This area once housed all the Government offices, the residential and administrative palaces, the ceremonial temples, altars and stelae and a ball court," he said. "Tikal was an extremely important religious, cultural and commercial centre. All the buildings would have been painted red with decorations superimposed in other colours. The tall flat façades on the tops of the temples are thought to have been painted with huge brightly coloured portraits of the faces of royalty, high priests and gods. In contrast, all paths, patios and squares were covered in white paving. The buildings date from between about 800 BC and 900 AD."

Lucas took us through to the Grand Plaza. On either side, stelae were placed on the flat grass area in front of towering temples rising far more steeply than those we had seen in Mexico. On the eastern side was the Temple of the Great Jaguar, more than one hundred and fifty feet high with a precipitous central staircase. The temple building at the top had a central portal and high steep roof and above this rose the remains of a façade nearly twice the height of the temple building.

"The Temple of the Great Jaguar was erected in the 8th century to hold the tomb of King Moon Double Comb, who was also known as Ah Cacao or Lord Chocolate," said Lucas. "He died in 734 AD and his burial treasures included stingray spines which were used in ceremonial bloodletting, as well as jade and pearls. The slightly lower temple on the other side of the Great Plaza, nearly one hundred and twenty five feet high, was also erected for Lord Chocolate and is known as the Temple of the Masks. During religious and civic ceremonies, incense would have been burned in the temples and human sacrifices would often take place."

Nobody was climbing the steps to the Temple of the Great Jaguar and we later found out from Peter that the guides discouraged this because visitors had actually slipped and fallen to their deaths. The Temple of the Masks was in a different design and had a staircase of about fifty steps jutting out in front of the pyramid into the Grand Plaza. This led to the top of the third tier where there was a wide ledge to walk around. Because these steps extended further into the Plaza, they were less steep and there were several tourists standing on the platform. A further flight of about ten steps led up between two shallower tiers to the temple on top which had an even higher, more impressive facade above its roof.

On the north side of the Plaza were two rows of stelae which, Lucas told us, recorded the history of the rulers of Tikal. Behind these was a flight of steps which we climbed but we were only part of the way up when we were caught in a short, sharp tropical shower with enormous raindrops that each seemed to be nearly an inch across. We sat on the steps, sheltering under our umbrellas until the rain stopped. The pools of water steamed on the hot stones and dried up completely within minutes. This reminded Lucas to tell us about the water supply for the city. "There were originally thirteen reservoirs in and around the city with rainwater ducted into these," he said.

When we reached the top of the steps, we were in the Northern Acropolis and Lucas showed us some temples where the outer layer of walling had fallen away to reveal another layer underneath. "The Mayans used an onion method of building," he told us. "It was common practice to build over the top of existing structures, one layer covering another like an onion skin, because they believed that the power of earlier temples and burial chambers was aggregated in temples built over them. The oldest structures here date back to about 400 BC."

"At the time of Lord Chocolate," Lucas continued, "the Northern Acropolis had twelve temples on a large platform. As in other Mayan complexes, some temples were aligned to the Sun at the time of the March and September solstices while others were aligned to the Sun at the time of the June and December solstices."

On the north side of the Plaza, some steps led down into a chamber that had once been built over but had been opened up. Part of the wall was missing which let in the light. Lucas took us down the steps and asked us to turn round. Facing us was an enormous stone mask about seven feet high with a hook nose and huge square ears and wearing a hat. "Now that's what I call impressive," said Sam. "I think it looks menacing," said Cheryl with a shudder. I was inclined to agree with her.

We now left the Northern Acropolis and returned to the Grand Plaza in the Central Acropolis. As we crossed between the Temple of the Great Jaguar and the Temple of the Masks to the south side, Lucas told us, "The palace was on this side of the Plaza and it is thought that Mayan noblemen also lived here in five storey buildings that were connected by passages and steps. Three storeys of each of these buildings are buried underground and the top floor has crumbled away, so what you can see are the remains of the fourth floor." In front of us rose a steep grass bank on top of which was a row of separate single storey buildings, reached by a narrow flight of steps cut into the bank. "It's very expensive to clear the jungle from the ruins," Lucas explained, "but it's more time-consuming and difficult to keep them cleared so it's better to preserve them underground."

From here, Lucas took us to a less developed part of the site known as the Lost World. He showed us a hill covered with forest, the trees growing out of stony ground. "Under this is a pyramid which has not been restored," he told us. "A thick layer of soil has been built up from plants rotting for more than a thousand years and tree roots grow in this soil, through and between the stonework." It made us wonder how any of these sites was ever discovered.

We now came to a pyramid that had been cleared but not restored, so the walls and steps were all very uneven and crumbling. "This is the Great Pyramid," said Lucas. "It is the oldest known structure in Tikal, built over other pyramids, the earliest of which dates back to about 700 BC. Although it's only about a hundred feet high, it's the largest in bulk of all the pyramids here. You are now standing in the south west corner of the Lost World Grand Plaza and this pyramid formed part of an astronomical complex."

"Although the ancient Mayans had discovered the wheel," he went on, "they had no form of transport. A wide band was placed round the forehead for pulling heavy loads and ramps were used to pull the stones up the pyramids. Small construction steps were used during building and these were later covered by large steps, each about eighteen inches high, although sometimes a narrow flight of small steps was left at one side. These small steps would be used by commoners while the large steps were for important people like the priests and Royal Family. The Mayans had good nutrition and are said to have been a well built race with an average height of about six foot but even so, they would not have been able to climb the steps at more than a stately pace." At the foot of the Great Pyramid were stelae with circular stones in front of them. "Those are altars," he told us.

From the Lost World Grand Plaza, we could see the upper part of another pyramid towering above the tree canopy. Lucas pointed it out and told us, "That is the Temple of the Double Headed Serpent. It is two hundred and thirty feet high and is the highest standing structure in Tikal. It was built in about 740 AD for Yaxkin Caan Chac, the son of Lord Chocolate. I shall take you there now along a jungle path." "Do you think there's any chance of seeing a quetzal?" asked Sue. "There are still quetzals in Guatemala but they are only found on higher ground in the centre and south of the country," he replied. "There are unlikely to be any round here."

Just as we set off, Garry spotted a fox sitting in the long grass by the trees and pointed him out to the rest of us. The fox did not seem too concerned by our presence but once he knew we had seen him, he stood up and slowly strolled into the forest.

At first, there was only room for us to walk in single file down the narrow jungle path and the cicadas were making a deafening noise that sounded exactly like chain saws cutting through logs. Then the path widened out and Lucas pointed out a dark bird, about the size of a blackbird, sitting on the branch of a tree. "That's a monarch bird, recognisable by its song." It was silent at the time and I wondered if its song was as beautiful as that of a blackbird.

I was actually far more intrigued by the lines of leaf-cutter ants which were carrying pieces of cut leaf back to their nest to feed a fungus, which in turn feeds the ants. Rather than dragging the leaf cuttings, the ants held them aloft as they scurried along. When a piece of leaf fell to one side, the tiny ant struggled to pull it upright again, so it could continue on its way. As each leaf section was many times the size of the little ant, the amount of strength required for this feat was unimaginable.

After only a few minutes, we reached the Temple of the Double Headed Serpent. Its height was equivalent to that of a twenty-three storey building and it could only be climbed by step ladders up the side of a precipitous, nearly vertical hill, as the majority of the temple was still buried under the mound. We could just glimpse the top of the temple between the foliage of the trees and we were all given the chance to climb to the top platform.

"Are you coming up?" I asked David. "It's too hot and I'm feeling tired," he said. "There's a water vendor over there so I'll buy another bottle and find somewhere to sit in the shade until you come down again." As I started climbing, he was chatting to Lucas and Peter who had climbed the temple before.

I was determined to see everything so I set off up the ladders but stayed behind everyone else, so that I could rest frequently. There were steep muddy stretches between the ladders that were quite slippery underfoot and I was a little worried about how I would cope with these on the way back down again. As I kept stopping for breath and another drink of water, I began to wonder whether I was being sensible in going higher and whether I had the energy to get to the top. I eventually managed it, however, and the view was breathtaking.

Up here, we could see for miles over the jungle canopy while here and there, in various directions, the tops of Mayan temples rose above the foliage. I felt it had been well worth the effort but by the time I was back on the ground, I was glad there were no more pyramids to be climbed that day.

After the tour ended, we had free time to wander around the ruins until 2 pm. We were then driven to our hotel which was very close to the site. The reception area, lounge, restaurant and a small shop were in a thatched complex on a hill and from here, paved paths led down through the rainforest to the accommodation, arranged in individual bungalows with reed thatched roofs, each with its own shower, washbasin and toilet.

David and I wheeled our cases down to our room and collapsed on the bed exhausted. After an hour's rest and a drink of water, we made our way up to the restaurant where we had a very late lunch of fresh pineapple. We then felt fully revived and explored the complex, following the fearsome roaring of a solitary howler monkey until we spotted him high up in the tree canopy.

According to the map Peter had given us, there was a craft market not far away so we set off to find it. On the way, we saw another black cicada on a palm leaf – I had my eye in now - and a beautiful multicoloured bird that looked as though it may be related to a peacock. Its head was orange with a white neck and green collar; its wings were banded green at the top, red in the centre and white at the bottom with black tips; and its breast and upper body were dark grey, the feathers down its back having increasingly wide bands of orange and blue, extending into longer tail feathers with orange and blue tips. Looking it up later, we discovered that this was an ocellated turkey, a wild bird also known as the Peten turkey.

A woman sat at the side of the steps at the entrance to the craft market, a pair of scissors and a selection of different coloured threads at her feet, embroidering a white cloth stencilled with Mayan designs. Several other women sat on low stools or mats on the ground around the edge of the market weaving on hand looms, much longer than those we had seen in Oaxaca. Balls of different coloured yarns lay beside them and they were producing the designs from memory. The top pole of each loom was tied to a post on the market stall, while the bottom pole was tied to a cord round the weaver's hips to control the tension. These two poles held the warp threads which were separated by further wooden poles, adjusted as needed when the yarn was passed through, to create the pattern.

We met Cheryl and Lynn in the craft market and as usual, they had been unable to resist making a few purchases. They had each bought a lovely woven suitcase which gave them plenty of extra packing space for blankets, curtains, tablecloths and runners. "Alan and I are getting married in September and setting up home from scratch, so I'm buying for our new home as well as collecting holiday souvenirs," said Lynn. "The main problem is trying to choose colour schemes so I've roped in Cheryl to help me." "It's difficult," agreed Cheryl. "There are just so many colour combinations and designs to choose from."

We left them to continue making their selections and looked for our own souvenirs. Some of the embroidery was exquisite with lovely designs in jewel colours but we were unable to picture the fabrics anywhere in our own home so we resisted the temptation to buy.

Next to the craft market was the local museum with a scale model of Tikal outside. Inside were the best of the carvings and stelae from the site but as usual in museums, flash photography was not allowed. After wandering around looking at these we were feeling tired again, so we sat in a nearby café enjoying a cool drink and a rest before heading back to the hotel.

As we set off again, we saw most of the group coming towards us led by Peter. "We're on our way back to the ruins to watch the sun set from the top of one of the pyramids," he said. "Come and join us."

Climb up the Temple of the Double headed Serpent, Tikal

View from the Temple of the Double Headed Serpent

Craft market, Tikal

Accommodation, Tikal

I pictured the long hill climb through the jungle. "I'm sorry," I said. "I would love to come but I just haven't got the energy." "You come along, then, David," encouraged Neville. "No, I need to go back and rest as well. Tell us about it in the morning."

We watched our friends hurrying towards the site and agreed that we both simply felt too exhausted to walk more than a mile uphill to the ruins, climb another pyramid and then walk more than a mile back in the dark down a slippery jungle track, exciting though it would have been.

That evening, the hotel generator was playing up and when we collected our key from Reception, we were told that instead of having power from 5.30 pm until 11 pm, it would only be available from 6.30 pm until 8.30 pm when the generator would be shut down for repairs. This was not a problem. We went for dinner at 7 o'clock and afterwards had a very early night and a well deserved rest.

Friday 11th July

We were woken at 4am the next morning by a scuffling noise and the sound of something dropping on the roof. "It's probably monkeys," said David. "Go back to sleep," but I found this impossible. Trying not to disturb David too much, I showered and dressed and went out as the first glimmers of dawn began to lighten the sky.

There was nothing to see on the roof by that time. I had hoped to spot some wildlife but, apart from a bat and a few early birds silhouetted against the sky, it was still too dark to see anything. A young couple came down the path and greeted me. "We're heading out to the ruins to see the sunrise," they said. "Come with us," I thought about it for a second or two but it was cloudy and I doubted whether the clouds would lift in time. The walk would also take about half an hour in each direction, we were leaving that morning after breakfast and I still needed to finish packing, so I thanked them for the invitation but declined.

I was nervous about venturing into the jungle alone so I wandered round the paths within the complex until 6.30 am. By this time, David was up so, as soon as we were ready, we took the cases to Reception, before going in for breakfast at 7 o'clock. Over the meal, our friends excitedly told us about the previous evening.

"We went back to the Grand Plaza and went up the steps to the Northern Acropolis," said Sue, "It was too cloudy to see the sunset but at dusk we saw a pair of toucans and a flock of green parrots." "Some coati mundis came up the steps to within a few feet of us," added Lynn. She was interrupted by Graham. "As we were leaving, we were attacked by a gang of monkeys. They thought we were invading their territory and they were hurling branches at us from the trees." "One of them hit me," said Ian. "We all ran back to the Plaza until they had gone." "Before we walked back in the dark, we could see the fireflies among the ruins," said Sue. "It was wonderful."

Immediately after breakfast, the luggage was loaded and we left Tikal. We first drove back to Lake Peten Itza and from here we took the road to Belize. Between Tikal and Flores, there was a good tarmac surface but the road then deteriorated to the usual stone and gravel track. From Flores, it was a further hundred kilometres to the border and as we drove through a very rural part of Guatemala, our driver had to watch out for dogs, ducks, pigs and chickens on the road.

7

BELIZE

We arrived at Melchor de Mencos on the Guatemalan border and this time, we all had to get off the coach and queue to show our passports in the Customs shed. We then walked through the shed, crossed the border and got back on the bus, which had been checked in the meantime and allowed to proceed. The same thing happened at the Belizean border a short distance down the road. Between the two borders, we passed a row of money changers and a shanty town selling food, drinks and souvenirs. At this point, the border was marked by the Rio Belize, a muddy brown river swollen by recent storms.

The rain set in as we entered Belize but, from the border, the road had a tarmac surface which gave us a much smoother ride. Although Guatemalans once considered Belize to be part of their territory, the first indications were that it was a far more prosperous country.

After only eleven kilometres, we reached San Ignacio. "We're going to stop here for half an hour," Peter told us. "It will give you the opportunity to experience a small town in Belize." As we walked down the main street, the first thing David and I noticed was that all the signs were in English and we soon discovered that everybody spoke English. We took advantage of this by asking the way to the local post office and buying a selection of Belizean stamps, to add to the Mexican and Guatemalan stamps we had already purchased as souvenirs.

The main roads through the town were surfaced with tarmac and the property styles were a mixture of wooden colonial and modern concrete. The old colonial houses had a great deal of character with attractive covered first floor balconies and roofs that overhung well beyond the walls to give protection from the weather. These were interspersed with concrete buildings, some of which also had covered first floor balconies, often with arched openings. The shops were generally small and specialist but there were two or three hotels.

The side roads, not surprisingly, were of sand and gravel but were generally in quite good condition. Many houses had small gardens protected by stone walls, wooden fencing or chicken wire. A few had high metal security fencing and metal grilles covering the windows which we had not seen elsewhere, indicating a problem with crime.

The people were also different. "In Mexico and Guatemala, most people are of Mayan descent but in Belize, only about 10% are Mayan, although back in the 7th century, Belize had a Mayan city that rivalled Tikal, with a population of about a hundred and fifty thousand," Peter told us, once we were back on the coach. "However, during the 9th century, the Mayans moved north into the Yucatan peninsula and very few remained by the time Columbus arrived in 1540. Now, the majority of the people are Mestizos, of mixed Spanish and Indian blood, or Creoles from the mixed blood of British white settlers and Jamaican slaves."

He then explained further. "Although Belize was part of their empire, the Spaniards virtually abandoned it when they could find no evidence of gold or silver in the area. About a hundred years later, British loggers arrived to exploit the timber resources and they settled along the coast, bringing in slave labour from Jamaica. The Spaniards had been having problems with British pirate ships which were attacking the Spanish galleons bound for Europe, laden with treasure from the richer parts of South America. They were not exactly pleased when they suddenly woke up to the fact that the British had also invaded part of their territory. The Spaniards fought the British in the Battle of St George's Cay in 1798 and briefly captured the Cay which had been the main British settlement in Belize. However, the British loggers settled instead in what is now Belize City and the whole area around it eventually became known as British Honduras."

"Because labour was in short supply," he went on, "the loggers and their slaves had to work side by side and everybody was perceived as being equal. Mixed marriages were common and there was no racial or class prejudice. The country gained its independence in 1965 but Guatemala still claimed sovereignty and refused to recognise Belize as an independent state until as recently as 1991. Belize still depends on foreign aid, as it can't grow enough food to be self-sufficient. Its main export is sugar but it probably makes more from the illegal trafficking of marijuana, known locally as 'Belize Breeze'."

As we made our way from San Ignacio to the coast, we noticed that many gardens had neat hedges or fences around them and orchards were fenced off. The jungle had been cleared well back from the road and many houses were built up on piles, indicating seasonal flooding problems. Diane commented on the large number of Bible training schools and Pentecostal churches we passed.

"Belize is very tolerant of different religions," Peter told us. "The majority of people are Catholic but some cling to their traditional beliefs as they do in Mexico. Here, you will also find various other Christian religions plus Hindus, Muslims and Rastafarians. The Mennonites have a strong following in Belize. They are very recognisable because the women wear bonnets and old-fashioned dresses and the men wear overalls and straw cowboy hats." "Are the Mennonites the same as the Amish?" asked Diane. "I'm not entirely sure of the differences," said Peter, "but both sects like to live traditionally without any form of mechanisation or technology. They live in farming communities, use horses to plough their land and travel in horse-drawn carts. They tend to keep to themselves, organise their own schools and finances and speak their own language."

We reached Belize City early in the afternoon, by which time the rain had ceased. As we drove through the town centre, we saw large signs warning against drugs and urging the citizens to keep Belize clean and beautiful. We were taken straight to our hotel on the seafront where the luggage was unloaded, while Peter booked us in at Reception and handed out the room keys. "When you've taken your cases up to your rooms, meet me back here and we'll go to the hotel restaurant for lunch," he said.

The hotel consisted of three old buildings joined together, with corridors sloping up and down to connect the different levels, which made me feel slightly off balance. There were no lifts so we all had to carry our luggage up the stairs to our rooms on the second floor. After a quick wash, we went back down to the lobby and Peter took us along a passage and up to the first floor restaurant in another part of the building.

David and I each ordered a ham and cheese toasted sandwich and a coffee. Instead of the light snack we were expecting, the sandwich came between three thick slices of toast and was served with large helpings of chips and salad while the coffee came in a pint mug. "I can't eat all this," said David, looking shocked. "I think tonight, we'd better share one meal between us," I suggested.

Immediately after lunch at 3 pm, we all set off on an organised bus tour of Belize City. The tour was run by one of the characters of Belize, a retired sea captain, who wore his captain's uniform and drove an old open bus with a ship's bell on a rope, which he rang every few minutes. He gave a running commentary as we drove around the city, while I tried to photograph everything of interest as we went past. I had the back seat to myself, so I was able to slide from one side to the other.

"The first settlers here were British loggers, who floated their timber downstream to Belize Harbour at the mouth of Haulover Creek, a branch of the Belize River," said the Captain. "They called it Haulover Creek because they had to haul their animals, tools and everything else they needed across the water. Once they had sold their timber, these loggers spent most of the proceeds on rum. Belize City was built during the 19th century on a mangrove swamp and is said to have been constructed on a foundation of woodchips and rum bottles. By the 1880s, the population was about five thousand, most of these being Creole descendants of the white loggers and their Jamaican slaves. Because the city was built on a series of islands connected by bridges across the mangrove swamp, it was a very unhealthy place in which to live and malaria was rife. The swamps were eventually drained and built over."

The Captain told us that because Belize City is situated on the coast, it had taken the full force of hurricanes in 1931 and 1961. "The devastation caused by Hurricane Hattie in 1961 was such that the Government decided to build a new capital city inland, in the centre of the country," he said. "This purpose built capital is called Belmopan and the Government and many of the embassies moved there in the 1970s. Unfortunately, once the Government had left Belize City, drug related crime increased and it quickly became quite dangerous, particularly in the poorer parts. Make sure you don't go wandering around alone, particularly after dark."

We passed an unusual looking statue of Mr Isaiah Emmanuel Morter, a dark-skinned man wearing black shoes, a black suit, white shirt and black bow tie and holding a book. "Mr Morter was the first coconut millionaire in Belize," said our guide proudly. The statue stood on a high, cream coloured plinth with a band of red, black and green stripes round the centre, while below the stripes, a flag and a coconut palm leant towards each other.

The Supreme Court was a distinguished two-storey building, plastered in white with delicate-looking white painted wrought iron railings on either side of its dog-leg staircase and along the front of the first floor balcony, built out over an arcade. At the top of the stairs, two posts supported a platform, jutting out from roof level, on which stood an airy, elegant open clock tower.

The Post Office was housed in a colonial white wooden building with white carved wooden railings up the side staircase and along the front of the first floor balcony. In contrast, the Central Bank of Belize was a solid looking affair in a light coloured stone, with heavy wrought iron grilles covering and protecting all its ground floor windows and with no outer staircase or balcony to provide easy access to the upper floor.

As we crossed the swing bridge, the Captain told us that this was the only working bridge of its kind left in the world. "It's opened manually every morning and evening to allow yachts and large boats through, holding up all the traffic and pedestrians in the process" he said. Below the bridge was Belize Harbour and looking towards the sea, we saw yachts moored on either side while a motor boat and canoe crossed the narrow stretch of water. It looked very attractive.

We went back to the coast past a flat open area of grassland. A central concrete path led to what looked like a small war memorial with a shelter behind it and the sea beyond. "The sea here is shallow for a long way out," the Captain told us, "and there are dozens of offshore islands known as cays, many consisting only of mangrove swamps. Beyond these is a barrier reef and then the ground suddenly drops away from the end of the continental shelf to a very great depth."

We came to a lighthouse, a slender, elegant construction within an enclosure, built on a platform with five steps leading up to it. "This is the Fort George Lighthouse and beside it is the tomb of a rich, eccentric Englishman, Baron Bliss," said our guide. "He came to Belize City at the end of his life in 1926 and anchored offshore in his yacht. He fell in love with Belize, despite never having set foot on land here and after only forty four days, he died on his yacht and left £1.6 million in trust to Belize City to build the tomb and lighthouse. The capital can't be touched and the interest from the trust fund must be used to benefit Belize and its citizens. It's already paid for the construction of a Performing Arts Centre, a School of Nursing, health centres and libraries and is also used to fund a Regatta each year on the date of the Baron's death."

He added, "This Regatta is one of the main annual events in Belize. It consists of a four day boat race down the Macal River which starts at San Ignacio - I believe you were there this morning - and it finishes in Belize City on Baron Bliss Day." "The Macal River joins the Belize River a few miles downstream from St Ignacio," clarified Peter.

Across the park near the lighthouse were some lovely old, white, wooden colonial buildings with white roofs, looking very picturesque.

Supreme Court, Belize City

Fort George Lighthouse

Mr Isaiah Emmanuel Morter

University, Belize City

View across the bay

From the seafront, we travelled up Fort Street and passed another impressive white building, this time with a plastered wall, steps leading up to a covered veranda that extended round at least two sides of the house and green shutters over the first floor windows. It was surrounded by lovely gardens with lawns, flowering shrubs and trees and it looked like an expensive private house. Outside, under the street sign painted in green lettering on a white background, hung a small notice reading 'Gift Shop'.

Because of the British founders, all the streets had English names. Once we had crossed the swing bridge, we had driven along Front Street, which ran beside the river and down to the seafront, while Regent Street lay on the other side of the river. The road leading to the bridge was Albert Street and that leading from the bridge was Queen Street. Victoria Street lay a little further inland. Houses were numbered according to their location in the city rather than where they stood on a particular road, so house numbers ran to several thousand.

As we drove along Queen Street, we passed the Queen's Bonded Warehouse, full of broken timbers with its roof hanging down from one corner. "It's in that state due to a combination of neglect and hurricane damage," the Captain told us. "There are two hazards here, hurricanes and fires. Several of our old timber buildings have been burned to the ground."

As we reached the outskirts of town, the Captain pointed out the drainage ditches running along both sides of the road. "Parents always warn their children never to play near the ditches," he said. "They are full of crocodiles."

This road took us past The University College of Belize. Two thirds of the cube-shaped three storey high entrance building consisted almost entirely of windows, reflecting the surrounding scenery like mirrors. The two storey wings stretching out on either side again consisted mainly of windows, separated by a band of concrete at top and bottom and along the centre. "There is also a West Indies University in the city," the Captain told us. "Education is seen as very important. It is free and compulsory from the age of six although many children attend kindergarten from the age of three."

We then drove round past the National Sports Complex which was still under construction, with a sign announcing that funds were being provided by Venezuela and promising a seating capacity of four thousand. From here, we headed back into the city.

"That's the Karl Hushner Hospital," commented our guide, ringing his bell as we came to another rather boxy looking building. "It was named after a Dr Hushner who was famous for his healing powers. The ambulances are all called BERT, the Belize Emergency Response Transport."

"Look at the palm trees in front of that house," said the Captain, pointing them out as we came back into a residential area. The long stems of the two palms, topped with fronded leaves, radiated out from the base of each of the plants in a quarter circle, like a pair of giant ostrich feather fans that had just been flipped open. "That type of palm has ten different names. These include the North-South palm, the finger palm, the fan palm and the Bird of Paradise palm."

We passed a well maintained park with a brightly painted perimeter fence in green, orange, blue and yellow, where the grass looked lush and green and children were playing on the swings. In contrast, another park that we passed looked rather neglected, with a rusting bandstand and large bare sandy patches in the grass.

On our way back towards the hotel, we came to a building with a red, white and green flag flying outside. "That's the Mexican Embassy," announced the Captain, noisily clanging his bell. The embassy was a handsome white wooden building with a red roof, red door and window frames, red awnings above the windows and with the edges of the steps and the balustrade painted red. On the opposite side of the road stood a convent, three storeys high and painted cream which, the Captain informed us, was rebuilt in 1942.

Finally, we went past St John's Cathedral, with a square tower at one end and windows reaching to the top of the tower. "This is the oldest Anglican cathedral in Central America, dating back to the 1800s," the Captain told us. "It was built of bricks brought over as ballast by ships from England."

The tour lasted two hours and was excellent. Since we had limited time in the city and it was unsafe to visit many areas, this was the best way to see the sights. As we returned to the hotel, pelicans were circling the bay and a tropical storm was brewing. The rain began to fall as we hurried inside.

We made our way up to the first floor restaurant which overlooked the bay. Here we bought drinks from the bar and sat watching the storm lash the shore. The windows had louvres which were designed to let in the air and keep out the rain but we had to sit well away from them as the wind forced the rain upwards and inside. The floor was soon quite wet.

Peter took this opportunity to give some advice to those of us who would be leaving for the airport later the following day and would have time to go exploring by ourselves in the morning. "Make sure you keep to the main roads and beware of touts selling boat trips," he warned. "They will ask you to pay them and will give you what looks like a legitimate ticket, specifying the name of the boat and the time it departs. However, when you arrive for the trip, you find that both it and the boat are non-existent. Also, if you walk along the front, you will probably be approached by drug dealers. They are very persistent and I've found that the best way to handle them is to say that you have already purchased a supply." All this made us very wary.

That evening, we had our last group dinner. The hotel was run by a Belizean woman married to a Scotsman and they had done their best to make it a special celebration meal. They had allocated us a private dining room on the ground floor with dark oak panelled walls and a long dining table, which they had decorated with flowers and candles.

Here we were served a delicious meal of pork chops cooked with sage, onion, apple and spices accompanied by jacket potatoes, carrots, broccoli and squash, followed by coconut tart made with fresh coconuts and cream. Wonderful! After coffee was served, it was suggested that we might like to attend the karaoke evening in the first floor bar-restaurant.

We discovered that this event was very popular with the young locals who had dressed up for it in jazzy shirts and the most miniscule of backless dresses. Our friends encouraged each other to take a turn. After about half an hour, Garry bravely went up to the front, took the microphone and gave a slightly off-key rendering of "I Did It My Way." We clapped and cheered him loudly.

Sue was trying to persuade Kayleigh to do a duet with her and after a few drinks to give her courage, Kayleigh reluctantly agreed. Their rendering of "Hey, Big Spender" was actually very good and it was difficult to believe that they had not practised the very professional-looking movements together beforehand. When David and I finally left at 1am and made our way to our bedroom, the party was still going strong. It had been an excellent way to spend a stormy evening.

Saturday 17th July

The sounds of the storm, crashing waves and howling winds that rattled the windows, continued for most of the night but had quietened down by the time we met the rest of the group for breakfast. Neville, Diane and Kayleigh, Sue and Ian were continuing the tour with Peter in the Yucatan Peninsula and we waved them off as they left in their taxis for the airport at 8.30 am. They were followed not long afterwards by Cheryl and Sam who were going to spend a few days relaxing on the Cays of Belize. Lynn and Alan would be leaving the hotel at 10.30 am for a flight to the Bahamas. Unfortunately, Garry, David and I all had to return to work on Monday and our holiday was nearly over. The three of us had the rest of the morning free in Belize City.

"We're going round the town," I said to Garry. "Would you like to come with us?" "Thank you but no, I've decided to have an easy morning relaxing in the hotel." Having said our farewells to Lynn and Alan, who were sitting and chatting with Garry in the lobby, David and I set off and wandered along the foreshore. The rain had stopped and the wind had died down but it was cloudy, warm and very humid. Instead of the calm blue sea we had seen on arrival, the water was brown with churned up sand and was still very choppy.

We crossed the swing bridge, heading towards the lighthouse, and found a shop with some lovely wooden carvings. We were very tempted by a marlin fish, but decided it was too large to carry. We found a heron with a slight flaw on one side, reduced to almost half price but although we loved it and it was a bargain, it would have been too awkward to transport home. We then found a carved, delicately shaped bowl in a dark polished wood with wonderful graining that was very reasonable. "That's beautiful," I said. "It would look lovely on the sideboard with fruit in it." "I like that as well," agreed David. "I can fit it into my rucksack for taking home."

We took it to the counter and the young girl wrapped it up with plenty of tissue paper for protection. "This bowl is made of zericote," she told us. "It's found in the dense rainforests of Belize and also on some of the offshore islands. It's one of the most popular hardwoods for carving because of its unique grain structure. Tourists love it." We certainly did.

As we left with our purchase, we saw a sign to a woodcarving workshop. "That might be interesting to visit," suggested David. We started walking down a side street towards it when we suddenly realised there was nobody around. "I don't like this," I said. "I think we ought to head back to the centre." Peter's warnings had left us feeling extremely nervous and we breathed a sigh of relief when we were back on the main road.

As we went towards the swing bridge, we were distracted by a hoarding near the Municipal Market with the warning in large red letters, "Consumer Beware of Cholera when you buy Apples, Grapes and Pears from Vendors on the Street Side. You are at Great Risk." People were urged to buy fruit from inside the market and to store purchases in a refrigerator. We did not want to go round the market so we went back across the bridge.

We continued down Albert Street where there were shops and plenty of people about. We were therefore surprised to be stopped by an armed police officer about a hundred yards down the road. "May I ask where you're going?" "Just to the end of the shops," I said. "I suggest you don't go any further than this," he warned us. "I cannot guarantee your safety beyond this point."

We were shocked and decided to head back to the hotel. This turned out to be a good decision as the sky was darkening and the pelicans were gathering in the bay. Just after we arrived back in the hotel, another tropical storm broke and continued until after we left Belize.

At midday, a taxi arrived to take Garry, David and me to the airport. When we reached the small departure lounge, Lynn and Alan were still waiting for their flight which had been delayed. We saw them off at 12.30 pm and as we hugged goodbye, they promised to send us some of their wedding photographs in due course.

Our own flight was on time although there were delays at Houston which meant that we had to run for our connection. Once on board the flight to England, we were then delayed for four hours, due to a faulty engine. We eventually reached Gatwick at 12.45 pm GMT (6.45 am Belize time) on Sunday and had lunch before driving home. We arrived at 6 pm, just over 24 hours since we had left our hotel in Belize. We were shattered but we had had some remarkable experiences and returned with wonderful memories of a fabulous holiday.

By the Same Author

From Coconuts to Condors

"They're going to throw those!" David said urgently. Carol was just assuring him that he was worrying unnecessarily when the first stones came hurtling across at the party. Our official City Guide immediately retaliated by picking up cobble stones himself and hurling them back at the youths..."

This was just one of many unexpected incidents, such as having to sleep in a blood-spattered hotel room or being served a meal of inedible llama meat followed by fizzy fruit salad, that made this trip to Brazil, Peru and Bolivia so unforgettable.

Reviews

David and Valerie Astill clearly have a gift for making friends... and were privileged to attend a number of local ceremonies and events such as the candomble in Salvador de Bahia, an important religious ceremony in honour of the gods, which very few tourists have experienced...Valerie Astill's descriptions of adventures, landscapes, costumes and local customs are detailed and picturesque. Her book also includes many photographs, sadly only in black and white.
Joan Stephens, Leicester Mercury

A nice travelog, honest and lightly written. It's warts and all, "The entrance and archway dating back to the 16th century had obviously been used more recently as a public convenience. It smelt dreadful..." If you want an insight into travel through Brazil, Peru and Bolivia, this will give you what you're after.
Paul Bondsfield, Explore Worldwide Ltd

As a fellow traveller to the Andes, I have much enjoyed 'From Coconuts to Condors'. I don't actually mind the photos being in black and white, as I can visualise the locations from Valerie's excellent descriptive writing. I have also enjoyed the fact that the book is well written, in the correct tense, and with proper punctuation! Having only been to Peru, I now want to visit both Brazil and Bolivia! Thank you Valerie.
Gill Twissel, author of 'Rest Upon The Wind'

We enjoyed this book because it conveys the reality of travel in these countries and the everyday issues facing the traveller. Too many travel books tend to present a 'tourist board' image of a location which is very different from the practical experience of the average visitor. Problems, hiccups and the unexpected help one to understand and appreciate a country much more. This is why the lack of colour photos doesn't matter. This book is a real journal of an exciting and challenging venture and not just a 'puff' for the South American tourism industry. Well worth reading.

Brian and Margaret Ludlow

ISBN 978-1-905809-57-8   £7.99

Available through any bookshop, on-line stores such as Amazon or Waterstones or direct from Publisher.